THE STORY OF
CIVILIZATION

VOLUME III
THE MAKING OF THE MODERN WORLD

TEACHER'S MANUAL

Illustrations by Chris Pelicano and Caroline K. Green

ISBN: 978-1-5051-0986-3

Printed and bound in the United States of America

THE STORY OF
CIVILIZATION

VOLUME III
THE MAKING OF THE MODERN WORLD

TEACHER'S MANUAL

TAN

Contents

THE MAKING OF THE MODERN WORLD

HOW TO USE THIS TEACHER'S MANUAL

Teaching History

History is at the core of any classical education. Engaging in the study of history gives a context for the world in which we live. Learning the great triumphs and failures of generations before us helps mold the decisions we make today. When taught in an engaging way, students can take the people and events of the past and relate them to their lives. It is an opportunity for the ultimate vicarious experience, and it can create a spark that will light the way for the next generation to solve problems, make discoveries, invent wondrous things, and inspire greatness.

Teaching Using the One-Room Schoolhouse Model

The *Story of the Civilization* is a wonderful text for teaching a single student or for teaching many students of varying grades all at one time. This text is designed to be used for grades 1–8.

If you are using this text with younger grades, you should revisit it again when the student is older. A classical education depends on laying a broad foundation at a young age that will be expanded upon later. Using *The Story of Civilization* twice will enhance the student's knowledge of history and allow for the addition of detail in later grades that was not committed to memory in early ones.

Using a schoolhouse model is not something seen in brick and mortar schools today, but it was the standard in the very recent past . . . and it worked. Some home schools utilize this method out of necessity or convenience, and some do so very intentionally because they find it to be a superior pedagogical method. Regardless of the reasoning, the one room schoolhouse model works and works well.

If you use the schoolhouse model, your older students might enjoy sitting in and following along in their own book while you read to the younger students. Older students then have the opportunity to review on their own. Going over Questions for Review as a group provides older students with a chance to help younger students with forgotten facts and provides younger students with the opportunity to show off what they know in front of older students. Impressing the parent/teacher is often not nearly as enticing as impressing an older sibling/older student. Likewise, learning something for your own sake may not be as enticing as sharing what you have learned with someone else.

If you are only using this text with students of the same age, the schoolhouse model can still be of great benefit. A little healthy competition can bring many children out of their shells and provide incentive for paying attention.

Using This Teacher's Manual

This Teacher's Manual is meant to work in conjunction with the Activity Book that goes along with *The Story of Civilization: Volume 3; The Making of the Modern World* series. The activities contained in this book are to be used after your student has completed the chapter of the textbook. The following is a list of sections you will find in this Teacher's Manual and the age range for which each section is appropriate:

QUESTIONS FOR REVIEW

This section is beneficial for the full range of elementary and middle school grades. For early elementary students, this section should be completed orally with lots of prompting and helpful hints. If you find the child struggling to come up with the answers independently, it may be most beneficial to both read the questions and provide the answers while engaging in discussion. Mastery of the answers should not be expected at these young ages. Exposure to the concepts is the key. For later elementary students, an oral evaluation is recommended. Expect MOST of the details to be provided by the student with minimal prompting. Oral answers should be given in complete sentences. For the middle school grades, a written evaluation would be ideal. Again, expect the student to provide MOST of the details. If you are teaching both elementary and middle school grades together, use the questions as an oral review for all, allowing the older students to aid the younger students with the details. Then use the questions as a written review for the older students. At this point, expect good written responses since the questions have been reviewed orally.

NARRATION EXERCISES

This section is most beneficial for the elementary aged student. Ask the student to provide you with a brief summary of the chapter. For the early elementary grades, expect knowledge of the basic storyline and provide any details that the child has omitted. For later elementary grades, the story line should be supplied by the student. An example has been provided for each chapter. This is just an example, not something that needs to be duplicated exactly by the student. You may want to have older elementary students keep a written account of their own responses. If desired, the teacher can produce and keep a written account for younger students.

MAP ACTIVITIES

This section is beneficial for the full range of elementary and middle school students. It is meant to provide a visual reference for the locations in which the stories take place. It is helpful to make use of a world map from time to time to remind the students of the overall world placement of the events before honing in on the particulars of the exact locale. This Teacher's Manual provides directions for each map activity. The maps are located in the Student's Activity Book under the chapter that corresponds with this text. You will find a map activity for almost every chapter.

ACTIVITY PROJECTS

There are a variety of Activity Projects found in this Teacher's Manual, each suited to different ages and interests. Please note that NOT all of the activities should be completed for each chapter. Choose the activities that will most engage your students, which will in turn fix the stories in their minds. Also note that a Materials at a Glance section has been added to the front of this manual so that you can gather your materials in advance without having to flip through each chapter. The possibilities of activities include:

COLORING PAGES

These are found in most chapters. Most of the pictures correspond with the pictures in the textbook. Visual representation for each chapter helps the student identify the events more clearly. Some coloring pages are purposefully designed to be more elaborate than a traditional coloring page. The lines aren't as clean, and there is a lot more detail. This makes these coloring pages ideal for the full range of elementary students as well as middle school students. Especially in the early elementary years, it is helpful to give out the coloring page before you begin reading the chapter. Allowing the child to work on the coloring page while the chapter is read keeps idle hands busy and brings to life the stories they are hearing.

WORD SEARCH / CROSSWORD PUZZLES / GAMES

These are designed for upper elementary and middle school students. If you have an early reader and proficient speller, younger students can attempt them, but their purpose is to provide a fun activity for the older students. The crossword or word search puzzles can be found in the Activity Book, and the answer key is found in the corresponding chapters in this Teacher's Manual.

CRAFT PROJECTS

These are mostly designed for the elementary school age student, although older students may find them fun as well. Gauge your student's interest level in doing the crafts. *Do not force these crafts on uninterested students.* History is supposed to be fun, and these crafts are designed to support that idea, not become one more activity to have to do on top of all the other schoolwork! Directions for each craft can be found under the appropriate chapter.

DRAWING PROJECTS

These are designed for older elementary and middle school aged students. They require a higher level of dexterity than most younger students can accomplish. Step-by-step instructions with visual guides can be found in the Activity Book.

SNACK PROJECTS

Now who doesn't love a good snack? And in some cases a full meal? This section is for use by any age (including adults). The snack provides another link to the story studied and helps reinforce the chapter. Weeks or even months later when you ask for the story of Jericho and your student looks at you with a blank stare, you can say "remember the graham cracker walls and the gummy bears," and just like that the student can suddenly recount every detail.

SCIENCE PROJECTS

These are intended for upper elementary and middle school students. With a lot of help and supervision, early elementary students will also find these projects engaging. Again, the point is to reinforce the chapter and provide a hands-on project to help commit the stories to memory.

WRITING ASSIGNMENTS

There are a few writing assignments meant to make the student think about the chapter and put some of the information into his or her own creative wording. This is best accomplished with pen and paper by older students, however it may be fun for younger students to attempt orally.

DRAMA PROJECTS

A great way to remember what you have read is to act it out. The students place themselves in the story and, in doing so, are more apt to remember the entire storyline.

THE FIVE KEYS TO MAKING THE MOST OF THIS TEACHER'S MANUAL

1. *Remember, history is fun!* Keep the classroom mood light. Allow your students a little room to engage, ask questions, and participate in discussions. Students shouldn't read this subject in order to get it over with as quickly as possible. It's meant to lay a foundation for a love of learning. Whether your students are in elementary grades, in middle school grades, or a mixture of the two, this text in meant to engage them in deep thought. They are challenged to open their minds and stretch their imaginations; to travel back in time to trace the origins of the human race and of the universe itself! Please make sure the journey is a fun one.

2. *DO NOT, under any circumstance, attempt to do all the activities in this book!* It's simply too much. Pick the activities that you think will be most beneficial for your students and do those. If you find a chapter or two in which you think all the activities are doable and you find yourself with extra time on your hands, go for it. If you find that one week a coloring page and word search were all that could manage, don't beat yourself up. This curriculum is designed to be fun for both the student and the teacher.

3. *Be a passenger on the voyage.* If, as the teacher, you learn something new or are reminded on something that you almost forgot, let your students see that you too are growing in knowledge. Allow your own excitement of the stories to come out in your discussion with the students. The best way to engage your student is to be engaged yourself.

4. *Don't set the bar too high for younger students.* As parent-teachers, we are often tempted to expect too much of our children because we know they are capable of it. If you are using this text with early elementary students, you should revisit it when your children are older. Expose younger students to all that history has to offer but don't try to drill every detail into them.

5. *If you have older students, let them take on some of the responsibility.* Let them look through the coming weeks and make a list of the activities they are most interested in. Allow them to list out and gather the supplies. If there are younger students in the classroom as well, allow the older students to pick out activities that they can help the younger students complete. Taking an active role in choosing the activities helps the student take ownership over what is learned.

ACTIVITY MATERIALS AT A GLANCE

Chapter 1 ···

Snack Project: STAINED-GLASS WINDOW SUGAR COOKIES

Materials and Ingredients:

- ☐ Ready-made sugar cookie dough
- ☐ Multicolored hard candy
- ☐ Flour
- ☐ Parchment paper
- ☐ Rolling pin
- ☐ Template from Activity Book

Craft Project: SCULPTING A CRUCIFIX

Materials:

- ☐ Plastic knife or craft stick
- ☐ Clay or Play-Doh of any color
- ☐ Paper plate
- ☐ Toothpicks

Chapter 2 ···

Craft Project: A PAPER TOWEL TELESCOPE

Materials:

- ☐ Paper towel roll
- ☐ Acetate paper
- ☐ Acrylic paints
- ☐ Utility knife

Chapter 3

Snack Project: JELLY BEAN AND TOOTHPICK CHURCH

Materials:

☐ 16 toothpicks

☐ 9 jelly beans (any color)

Craft Project: PAPAL HAT

Materials:

☐ Tape
☐ Scissors

☐ Template from Activity Book

Chapter 4

Craft Project: BUILD A PAPER 3-D CASTLE

Materials:

☐ Scissors
☐ Glue

☐ Template from Activity Book

Chapter 5

Game: CHALLENGE GAME (2–4 PLAYERS)

Materials:

☐ Scissors
☐ Colored pencils

☐ Templates from Activity Book

Craft Project: SUGAR CUBE TOWER OF LONDON

Materials:

☐ Sugar cubes
☐ Frosting
☐ Plastic knife

☐ 10" × 10" cardboard base
☐ Foil

Craft Project: ST. THOMAS MORE CREST

Materials:

☐ Scissors
☐ Glue
☐ Colored pencils

☐ Templates from
   Activity Book

Chapter 6

Snack Project: QUEEN CATHERINE CROISSANTS

Materials and Ingredients:

- ☐ 1 tube of croissant dough
- ☐ Sandwich fillings of your desire (for example: ham and cheese, peanut butter and jelly, Nutella)
- ☐ 8 toothpicks
- ☐ Template of the French flag (3 mini flags)
- ☐ Scissors
- ☐ Colored pencils
- ☐ Tape
- ☐ Templates from Activity Book

Craft Project: JOUSTING SWORD

Materials:

- ☐ Large roll of gray or silver duct tape
- ☐ Yardstick
- ☐ Dark-colored washcloth

Chapter 7

Craft Project: QUEEN MARY'S CROWN

Materials:

- ☐ Small assorted craft jewels (or cut-out small shapes from colored construction paper)
- ☐ Glue
- ☐ Colored pencils or crayons
- ☐ Tape
- ☐ Template from Activity Book

Chapter 8

Craft Project: PAPER BISHOP'S STAFF

Materials:

- ☐ Piece of white copier paper
- ☐ Scissors
- ☐ Tape
- ☐ Black pen
- ☐ Ruler

Game: FIND CHARLES BORROMEO'S MUSKET BALL

Materials:

- ☐ 1 marble

Chapter 9

Snack Project: CHRISTIAN COOKIE SHIPS ON AN OCEAN OF JELL-O

Materials and Ingredients:

- ☐ Box of blue Jell-O
- ☐ Fruit leather cut into small triangle flags, about 1″ in length, one for each ship
- ☐ Clear glass baking dish
- ☐ 6–8 vanilla-, chocolate-, or strawberry-filled wafer cookies cut in half (these are the "ships")
- ☐ Toothpicks
- ☐ Scissors

Game: BATTLE OF LEPANTO BATTLESHIP

Materials:

- ☐ Templates from Activity Book
- ☐ Pencils

Chapter 10

Craft Project: PAPER ALTAR DIORAMA

Materials:

- ☐ Colored pencils
- ☐ Tape
- ☐ Scissors
- ☐ Glue stick
- ☐ shoe box
- ☐ Template from Activity Book

Chapter 11

Craft Project: PAPER PLATE SPANISH ARMADA SHIP

Materials:

- ☐ Paper plate
- ☐ Straws
- ☐ Paper
- ☐ Brown paints
- ☐ ½ of a paper towel roll
- ☐ Glue
- ☐ Scissors
- ☐ Stapler
- ☐ Pencil
- ☐ Markers
- ☐ Hole punch

Craft Project: KING PHILIP II'S COAT OF ARMS

Materials:

- ☐ Scissors
- ☐ Glue
- ☐ Template from Activity Book

Chapter 12

Game: THE THIRTY YEARS' WAR

Materials:

☐ Plastic army soldiers (2 colors, 10–20 or more of each color)

☐ 4 small, bouncy rubber balls

Game: THE THIRTY YEARS' WAR CARD GAME

Materials:

☐ Deck of 52 cards

Chapter 13

Snack Project: GUY FAWKES GUNPOWDER COOKIES

Ingredients:

☐ Package of premade sugar cookie dough
☐ Can of premade frosting

☐ 2–3 packages of Pop Rocks

Game: THE CROWN VERSUS PARLIAMENT CHECKERS

Materials:

☐ Colored pencils
☐ Scissors
☐ Tape
☐ Template from Activity Book

Chapter 14

Craft Project: WAX SEAL STAMP

Materials:

☐ Hot glue gun and glue
☐ Air-dry clay
☐ 1 tack pin
☐ Craft paints
☐ Parchment paper

Game: PUT OUT THE GREAT FIRE OF 1666

Materials:

☐ Poster board
☐ Poster-board paints or poster markers

☐ Water balloons
☐ Scissors

Chapter 15

Craft Project: KING LOUIS'S WIG

Materials:

☐ Old baseball cap or painter's cap
☐ Glue
☐ Cotton

Drama Project: THE SUN KING

Materials:

☐ Wig from the craft project "King Louis's Wig"
☐ Small container with powder
☐ Table with chairs
☐ Couch/bed

Snack Project: SACRED-HEART STRAWBERRIES

Materials and Ingredients:

☐ 12 strawberries
☐ Pineapple segments (canned or fresh)
☐ Chocolate frosting in a tube, small tip

☐ 24 toothpicks
☐ 12 mini marshmallows

Chapter 16

Craft Project: WINGED HUSSARS BROWN PAPER BAG PUPPET

Materials:

☐ Glue
☐ Scissors
☐ Colored pencils

☐ Standard-size brown paper lunch bags
☐ Red marker
☐ Templates from Activity Book

Snack Project: EDIBLE KNIGHT

Materials and Ingredients:

☐ Pringles
☐ Tostitos Scoops

☐ Mandarin orange slices
☐ Licorice

- ☐ Green peppers
- ☐ String cheese
- ☐ Knife
- ☐ Plate

Chapter 17

Craft Project: FLOATABLE BOAT

Materials:

- ☐ 2 wine corks
- ☐ Toothpick
- ☐ Cereal box
- ☐ Hot glue gun
- ☐ Scissors
- ☐ Tape

Chapter 18

Craft Project: HOMEMADE TELESCOPE

Materials:

- ☐ Rubber band
- ☐ Tissue paper
- ☐ Empty cardboard paper towel roll
- ☐ Paint
- ☐ Paintbrushes
- ☐ Glue
- ☐ Confetti stars

Snack Project: EDIBLE LEANING TOWER OF PISA

Materials and Ingredients:

- ☐ Recipe for Rice Krispies Treats
- ☐ Frosting
- ☐ Pie pan
- ☐ 1 wooden kitchen skewer (cut in half)
- ☐ White paper
- ☐ Toothpick
- ☐ Scissors
- ☐ Colored pencils
- ☐ Round cookie cutter
- ☐ Tape

Science Project: TESTING GRAVITY

Materials:

- ☐ Basketball
- ☐ Marble
- ☐ Baseball cap
- ☐ Large sofa cushion
- ☐ Paper clip
- ☐ Tennis shoe

Chapter 19

Craft Project: GEORGE WASHINGTON MASK

Materials:

- ☐ Scissors
- ☐ Tape
- ☐ Glue
- ☐ 2 craft sticks
- ☐ Cotton balls
- ☐ Markers
- ☐ Red, white, and blue construction paper
- ☐ Templates from Activity Book

Game: BATTLE OF QUIBERON BAY BOWLING

Materials:

- ☐ 16 clothespins (the kind that you squeeze to open)
- ☐ Colored pencils
- ☐ Scissors
- ☐ Small, bouncy rubber ball
- ☐ Templates from Activity Book

Chapter 20

Craft Project: CRAFT STICK CRUCIFIX

Materials:

- ☐ Colored pencils
- ☐ Scissors
- ☐ Glue
- ☐ 2 craft sticks
- ☐ Template from Activity Book

Craft Project: CANNON MARSHMALLOW SHOOTER

Materials:

- ☐ Scissors
- ☐ Sturdy single-serve yogurt cup
- ☐ Balloon
- ☐ Mini marshmallows

Chapter 21

Craft Project: NAPOLEON'S HAT

Materials:

- ☐ 2 6"x18" long pieces of felt
- ☐ Scissors
- ☐ Tape
- ☐ Craft glue
- ☐ Template from Activity Book

Snack Project: NAPOLEON SANDWICH COOKIES

Ingredients:
- ☐ Graham crackers
- ☐ Whipped cream
- ☐ Strawberries

Chapter 22

Snack Project: ORPHANAGE OAT-AND-FRUIT BOWL

Ingredients:
- ☐ 1 cup of vanilla yogurt
- ☐ 1 crunchy granola bar
- ☐ Blueberries
- ☐ Raspberries

Chapter 23

Craft Project: THE REFORM BILL SCROLL

Materials:
- ☐ Large brown paper bag
- ☐ Markers
- ☐ Ruler
- ☐ String
- ☐ Scissors
- ☐ 2 unsharpened pencils
- ☐ Tape

Snack Project: EDIBLE CORN LAWS

Materials and Ingredients:
- ☐ Write-on piping frosting (any color but white)
- ☐ Paper plate
- ☐ Popcorn (already popped)

Chapter 24

Game: MORSE CODE GAME

Materials:
- ☐ Flashlight
- ☐ Paper
- ☐ Pencil
- ☐ Template from Activity Book

Snack Project: EDIBLE RAILROAD

Materials and Ingredients:

☐ Graham crackers
☐ Canned frosting
☐ Black licorice ropes

☐ 2′ × 2′ cardboard (size may vary)
☐ Foil

Chapter 25

Craft Project: PRAYER TO ST. MICHAEL SHIELD

Materials:

☐ White poster board
☐ Pencil
☐ Markers (various colors)

☐ Scissors
☐ Ruler

Craft Project: SWISS PONTIFICAL GUARD DRUM

Materials:

☐ Container (such as an oatmeal or ice cream tub)
☐ Yarn
☐ Packing tape
☐ Chopsticks
☐ Craft foam

☐ Markers
☐ Butcher paper
☐ Scissors
☐ Ruler

Craft Project: ST. MICHAEL'S FLAMING SWORD

Materials:

☐ Orange and red markers
☐ Tape
☐ A wooden yardstick
☐ A 6″ or 12″ wooden ruler

☐ Duct tape
☐ Glue
☐ Scissors
☐ Template from Activity Book

Chapter 26

Craft Project: MAKE A CHINESE HAT

Materials:

☐ Large sheet of colored poster board
☐ Scissors
☐ Tape

☐ Glue
☐ Markers

Snack Project: BRITISH CANDY BOATS ON THE YANGTZE RIVER

Materials and Ingredients:

- ☐ Candied fruit slices
- ☐ Toothpicks
- ☐ Colored pencils
- ☐ Tape
- ☐ 1 tub Cool Whip
- ☐ Blue food coloring
- ☐ Templates from Activity Book

Chapter 27

Craft Project: WORLD WAR I AIRPLANE

Materials:

- ☐ Cardboard pieces
- ☐ 1 empty toilet paper roll or paper towel roll cut in half
- ☐ Scissors or utility knife
- ☐ Glue
- ☐ Colored markers
- ☐ Templates from Activity Book

Craft Project: THE BRITISH TRENCHES

Materials:

- ☐ Medium-size cardboard box
- ☐ Toothpicks
- ☐ Craft sticks
- ☐ Glue or tape
- ☐ Mud or potting soil
- ☐ Twigs from outside
- ☐ Plastic army men (optional)

Chapter 28

Craft Project: TREATY OF VERSAILLES DOCUMENT

Materials:

- ☐ Brown paper bag
- ☐ Black marker
- ☐ Scissors

Craft Project: MAKE A MINI FASCES

Materials:

- ☐ 1 dowel, ½" diameter and about 1 ½' long
- ☐ 9–12 dowels, ¼" diameter and about 1' long
- ☐ Hot glue gun
- ☐ Red ribbon
- ☐ Small piece of cardboard
- ☐ Scissors
- ☐ Tape
- ☐ Silver spray paint

Chapter 29

Craft Project: PAPER ARMY TANK

Materials:

- ☐ Scissors
- ☐ Glue
- ☐ Colored markers or pencils

- ☐ A piece of construction paper (any color)
- ☐ Template from Activity Book

Snack Project: CANDY TANK

Materials and Ingredients:

- ☐ 6 mini Reese's Peanut Butter Cups, wrapped
- ☐ Tootsie Roll Pop, wrapped

- ☐ 2 mini Hershey candy bars, wrapped
- ☐ 3 Twix candy bars, wrapped
- ☐ Tape

Chapter 30

Craft Project: MAXIMILIAN KOLBE FIGURINE

Materials:

- ☐ Ping-pong ball
- ☐ Toilet paper roll
- ☐ Black and white poster paint

- ☐ Brown and black Sharpie markers
- ☐ Tape or glue

Craft Project: PARACHUTE FOR TOY ARMY MAN

Materials:

- ☐ Plastic grocery bag
- ☐ String or yarn
- ☐ Scissors

- ☐ Ruler
- ☐ Toy army man

Chapter 31

Craft Project: ARMY DOG TAG

Materials:

- ☐ Rectangular key chain
- ☐ String or yarn
- ☐ A small photo of yourself
- ☐ Glue
- ☐ Scissors

Snack Project: A CANDY BERLIN WALL

Materials:

☐ Mamba candies
☐ Vanilla frosting

☐ Paper plate

Craft Project: ARMY NURSE HAT (FOR GIRLS)

Materials:

☐ Tape or glue stick
☐ Scissors
☐ Red marker

☐ Template and folding instructions from Activity Book
☐ 8.5x11 sheet of white paper

Chapter 32

Craft Project: MINI 1950S TELEVISION SET

Materials:

☐ An empty Keurig box or similar (the smallest size)
☐ 4 clip-on clothespins
☐ 2 twist ties
☐ Scissors

☐ Tape
☐ Brown poster paint
☐ Black Sharpie marker
☐ Any small picture to fit into the television screen

Craft Project: HANDMADE TELEPHONE

Materials:

☐ 2 Solo plastic cups
☐ 7–10 feet of yarn

☐ Scissors
☐ 2 paper clips

Chapter 33

Snack Project: GIANT RICE KRISPIES TREAT BISHOP'S MITER

Materials and Ingredients:

☐ Rice Krispies treat recipe
☐ Wax paper
☐ Knife
☐ Ruler
☐ Premade can of white cake frosting (1 or 2 cans)
☐ Yellow food coloring

Chapter 34

Snack Project: TWIX CANDY BERLIN WALL

Materials:

- ☐ Bag of mini Twix candy bars
- ☐ Frosting
- ☐ Paper plate
- ☐ Sharp cutting knife or meat mallet

Craft Project: POPE JOHN PAUL II PAPER BAG PUPPET

Materials:

- ☐ White paper lunch/craft bag
- ☐ Scissors
- ☐ Glue
- ☐ Yellow and red markers
- ☐ Template from Activity Book

Chapter 35

Craft Project: CATECHISM OF THE CATHOLIC CHURCH MINI BOOK

Materials:

- ☐ 8 ½″ × 11″ copy paper
- ☐ Scissors
- ☐ Colored pencils

Craft Project: HOLY WATER FONT

Materials:

- ☐ A small, plain rectangular wooden plaque
- ☐ Sawtooth picture hanger
- ☐ Hammer
- ☐ Clear plastic shot glass
- ☐ School glue
- ☐ Hot glue gun and glue sticks
- ☐ Holy card picture

CHAPTER 1
THE GLORY OF THE RENAISSANCE

QUESTIONS FOR REVIEW:

1. **The Italian Renaissance took place during what years?**
   1400s and 1500s.

2. **When wealthy people would pay for famous artists to decorate their cities, it was called what?**
   Patronage.

3. **What stone carving made Donatello famous?**
   The Annunciation.

4. **What did Brunelleschi carve in order to "compete" with Donatello?**
   A crucifix.

5. **Besides Italians, what other artists contributed to art in the Renaissance?**
   The Dutch and Flemish.

NARRATION EXERCISE:

Art in the Renaissance

The Renaissance of the 1400s and 1500s is sometimes known as the Italian Renaissance because its most notable artists were Italian. Artists of the Renaissance decorated Christendom with glorious paintings and sculptures, many of which still exist today. In the city of Florence, there lived two talented sculptors named Brunelleschi and Donatello. Once, they competed to see who could carve a more beautiful crucifix. But what really made Donatello famous was a stone carving he did of the Annunciation for the parish of St. Croce in Florence. In addition to Italian artists and sculptors, the Dutch and Flemish painted some of the most realistic art of the Renaissance. Like other artists, the Dutch and Flemish masters painted religious works, decorating churches and altar pieces. One of the most spectacular Dutch Renaissance paintings is the *Arnolfini Marriage* by Jan van Eyck. Done in 1434 on a large oak panel, it is considered one of the greatest paintings of the Renaissance.

WRITING ASSIGNMENT: RETELL THE STORY OF DONATELLO AND BRUNELLESCHI

In your own words, rewrite the story of Donatello and Brunelleschi. Then draw a picture to go with the story.

DOUBLE PUZZLE: THE DUTCH AND THE FLEMISH

(Activity Book page 5)

Unscramble the words from the section "The Dutch and Flemish." Copy the letters in the numbered cells to other cells with the same number to help answer the question.

The Dutch and Flemish painted some of the most realistic art of the _____.

Answer Key:

Recipe	Wonderful
Germany	Wife
Paint	Famous
Greece	Donatello
Flemish	Coast
Altar	**Renaissance**

RIEPEC — R E C I P E
RAYMENG — G E R M A N Y
TAIPN — P A I N T
CEGREE — G R E E C E
SIEFHLM — F L E M I S H
LATRA — A L T A R
REWDUNFOL — W O N D E R F U L
FEWI — W I F E
MAUFOS — F A M O U S
NEOLATDOL — D O N A T E L L O
SOCTA — C O A S T

SNACK PROJECT: STAINED-GLASS WINDOW SUGAR COOKIES

Materials and Ingredients:

☐ Ready-made sugar cookie dough

☐ Multicolored hard candy

☐ Flour

☐ Parchment paper

☐ Rolling pin

☐ Template from Activity Book *(Activity Book page 7)*

Instructions:

1. Cut along only the outer edge of cookie template.
2. Unwrap and separate hard candies by color.

3. Crush the candy to a fine consistency.

4. Roll out dough into ¼-inch thickness, using flour to prevent sticking.

5. Place on parchment-lined cookie sheet.

6. Using a knife, cut along the inside of the window (about the size seen in the interior of the template), following the lines of the template to make a small interior duplicate of the window, which you will fill in with crushed candy.

7. Reuse scraps of dough.

8. Bake according to instructions on the cookie dough package.

CRAFT PROJECT: SCULPTING A CRUCIFIX

Materials:

☐ Plastic knife or craft stick

☐ Clay or Play-Doh of any color

☐ Paper plate

☐ Toothpicks

Instructions:

1. Use the paper plate as a work surface and to easily transport the clay if needed.

2. Put a chunk of clay onto the paper plate for the student to carve a 3-D crucifix that can stand up on its own.

3. Use toothpicks to reinforce the crossbeams.

4. Make sure to create a clay base that is bigger than the bottom of the cross so it can stand upright.

COLORING PAGE: DONATELLO AND BRUNELLESCHI

(Activity Book page 9)

Color the picture of Brunelleschi presenting his crucifix to Donatello.

CHAPTER 2
COLUMBUS AND THE NEW WORLD

QUESTIONS FOR REVIEW:

1. **What were the names of Columbus's three ships?**
   Niña, Pinta, and *Santa María.*

2. **What did the king and queen promise Columbus if his trip was successful?**
   That he would become admiral and be made governor of any land he discovered.

3. **On what date did Columbus and his crew reach land?**
   October 12, 1492.

4. **Why did Columbus call the people of the new land "Indians"?**
   He thought he had gone around the world and landed in India.

5. **On what present-day islands had Columbus landed?**
   The Bahamas.

NARRATION EXERCISE:

The Journey of Columbus
Christopher Columbus was an experienced navigator who had traded along the coasts of Africa. He believed that the best way to get east was by sailing west. He brought his idea to King Ferdinand and Queen Isabella of Spain. They told him that if he succeeded, he would be given the rank of admiral and made governor of all new lands he might discover. Columbus was given three ships called the *Niña*, the *Pinta*, and the *Santa María*. They left Spain on August 3, 1492, sailing southwest across the broad Atlantic Ocean. For many weeks, they pressed on across the open sea with no sign of land. Finally, they arrived in what are now the islands of the Bahamas on October 12, 1492. They named the little island they landed on San Salvador, which means "Holy Savior" in Spanish. Columbus returned to Spain in March 1493. He presented Ferdinand and Isabella with birds, plants, fruits, and even some of the natives he brought back from his

voyage. Columbus would return to the Caribbean three more times, exploring many more lands. He received the rank of admiral and governorship of the new lands, as promised.

MAP ACTIVITY: THE ROUTE OF THE NIÑA, THE PINTA, AND THE SANTA MARÍA

(Activity Book page 11)

1. Find Spain on the map and draw three tiny ships besides its coastal border to signify that this was where Columbus and his crew left from on August 3, 1942.

2. Find the island of San Salvador in the Bahamas, where Columbus's crew landed, and draw three ships there.

3. Draw a dotted line between your two drawings to show the route Columbus took.

4. Find India on the map and circle it to show that this was where Columbus thought he had landed, which is why he called the natives "Indians."

MAZE: COLUMBUS SETS SAIL

(Activity Book page 12)

Instructions:
Help Columbus leave Spain and find his way to San Salvador!

DRAMA PROJECT: COLUMBUS AND HIS CREW

(Activity Book page 13) Act out the play with Columbus and his crew.

Materials:

☐ Sofa

☐ Telescopes from craft, "A Paper Towel Telescope" (optional)

CROSSWORD PUZZLE: COLUMBUS AND THE NEW WORLD

(Activity Book page 14)

Answer Key:

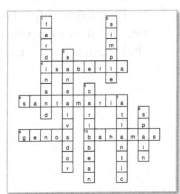

Across:

4. Isabella
6. Santa María
9. Genoa
10. Bahamas

Down:

1. Ferdinand
2. simple
3. San Salvador
5. Caribbean
7. Atlantic
8. Spain

CRAFT PROJECT: A PAPER TOWEL TELESCOPE

Materials:

☐ Paper towel roll
☐ Acetate paper
☐ Acrylic paints
☐ Scissors

Instructions:

1. Paint the paper towel roll any color you would like your telescope to be (or leave it as is).
2. Use the end of the paper towel roll to trace circles on the acetate paper, which will be used for slides to view in the telescope.
3. On top of each slide, draw a connected square that suffices as a handle used to insert the slides in and out of telescope.
4. Have a parent cut out slides with scissors.
5. Paint a scene inside the circle of the slide. Let dry. *Suggestion: simple landscape of hills, clouds, a bird, the ocean waves.*
6. From about 2 inches from one end of the telescope, cut a slit halfway down. This is where you will insert the slides.
7. Enjoy!

COLORING PAGE: CHRISTOPHER COLUMBUS

(Activity Book page 15)

Color the picture of Columbus and his three ships. Do you remember what they were called? Write their names beside each one.

CHAPTER 3
MARTIN LUTHER

QUESTIONS FOR REVIEW:

1. **Describe the sin of scandal.**

   Scandal describes the act of causing others to lose their faith because of something you did or said.

2. **What word means a mitigation or lessening of penance for sins already confessed?**

   Indulgence.

3. **Who did not believe in the authority of the pope and the teachings of the Church?**

   Martin Luther.

4. **Who issued the decree of the Edict of Worms?**

   Charles V.

5. **Why couldn't the emperor capture Luther for his crimes against the Church?**

   He went into hiding.

NARRATION EXERCISE:

Martin Luther

Martin Luther was an Augustinian monk and a theology teacher at the University of Wittenberg in Germany. He denied the authority of the Church and the power of the pope, even calling him an antichrist. Luther also denied the teachings of the Church, saying that every person should just read the Bible on their own and come up with their own meanings to the best of their ability. He believed that people did not need to do penance for their sins. He taught that faith alone—without anything else—was all that one needed to be saved. Pope Leo X heard of Luther's ideas and asked him to recant. He would not. The accused heretic was scheduled to appear before Emperor Charles V. Before Charles had a chance to announce his fate, Luther was gone. He fled the city and went into hiding. Luther would never be captured because he already had too many supporters who helped hide him. The storm Luther unleashed would soon turn violent and plunge Germany into chaos.

CRYPTOGRAM: DIFFICULT PENANCES

(Activity Book page 17)

During the Middle Ages, penances received in confession could be very hefty. One of them might be to _____. Read the section "Albert's Indulgences" to find the answer and help decode the cryptogram.

Answer: FAST FOR FORTY DAYS ON BREAD AND WATER

WORD SEARCH: MARTIN LUTHER

(Activity Book page 18).

Find all the words that have to do with the German monk-turned-heretic, Martin Luther.

Answer Key:

1. Albert
2. Leo
3. Luther
4. Charles
5. scandal
6. heretic
7. indulgence
8. Worms
9. Diets
10. penance
11. Bible

C	B	T	L	C	L	G	J	T	J	B	R	M	X	L
R	H	X	U	I	S	I	W	J	R	J	I	C	C	H
E	H	A	C	M	O	A	S	L	A	E	Q	B	E	H
H	U	H	R	E	C	N	A	N	E	P	B	R	L	F
T	U	O	X	L	D	I	E	T	S	D	E	L	F	E
U	W	H	B	V	E	S	E	L	Y	T	W	P	A	T
L	K	P	I	C	X	S	R	P	I	S	F	L	Z	F
R	B	C	G	V	C	W	O	C	J	C	J	P	U	Q
W	H	O	C	L	B	Z	T	Z	B	A	H	G	T	J
U	V	Y	G	D	X	K	U	T	P	N	Z	N	M	P
N	P	Q	K	Q	W	C	P	P	N	D	V	Q	F	V
I	N	D	U	L	G	E	N	C	E	A	O	O	I	F
U	H	G	H	W	L	X	U	T	R	L	K	C	U	Z
L	D	H	T	P	E	H	A	E	T	B	G	A	Q	G
L	P	V	F	F	O	M	V	O	S	W	K	U	B	X

SNACK PROJECT: JELLY BEAN AND TOOTHPICK CHURCH

Materials:

- ☐ 16 toothpicks
- ☐ 9 jelly beans (any color)

Instructions:

1. Connect a jelly bean to one end of a toothpick and repeat to form a square (a total of 4 toothpicks and 4 jelly beans).
2. Repeat step #1 to have a total of two squares.
3. Connect one square on top of the other using 4 more toothpicks to form a 3-D cube.
4. With the remaining 4 toothpicks, construct a slanted roof on top that is connected by one jelly bean on the top.
5. Show it to everyone, then eat it!

CRAFT PROJECT: PAPAL HAT

Materials:

- ☐ Tape
- ☐ Scissors
- ☐ Template from Activity Book *(Activity Book page 19)*

Instructions:

1. Cut out the template for the hat in the Activity Book. Decorate it.
2. Cut out a strip of paper that fits around the child's head. Attach it to the template.
3. Wear it!

COLORING PAGE: MARTIN LUTHER

(Activity Book page 21)

Color the picture of Martin Luther nailing his *95 Theses* to the door of the cathedral at Wittenberg in October 1517.

CHAPTER 4
GERMANY ON FIRE

QUESTIONS FOR REVIEW:

1. **What was the "spark" that caused chaos and violence in Christendom?**
   Martin Luther's revolt.

2. **Who preached some of Luther's ideas but, unlike Luther, believed in violence?**
   Thomas Müntzer.

3. **How did some Germans feel about the pope?**
   They wanted independence from his authority.

4. **Why was Luther angry with some of the peasants even though they admired him?**
   He thought they were twisting his words.

5. **How did Emperor Charles attain peace?**
   He summoned a meeting and told them they could choose to be Lutheran or Catholic.

NARRATION EXERCISE:

The Consequences of Luther's Actions
Martin Luther probably did not intend to throw all of Christendom into chaos. He also didn't think his questions about indulgences would lead to violence, but that's exactly what happened. There were many greedy nobles and knights who wanted the Church's lands. German peasants began to revolt against their lords. Though some peasants were admirers of Luther, he was very angry with them. Luther wrote a letter to the nobles of the kingdom, encouraging them to put down the rebellion. The nobles gathered their armies and began fighting back. The peasants were destroyed, and the revolt was quickly put down. But war would continue to plague Germany and the Holy Roman Empire for decades. Eventually, after

many years, Charles summoned a meeting of all the princes of his empire and said, "Each one of you can choose whatever religion you want for your kingdom. If you want it to be Lutheran, it shall be Lutheran. If you want it to be Catholic, it shall be Catholic." The fighting was over for now, but Germany was divided between Lutherans and Catholics.

WRITING ASSIGNMENT: A LETTER TO MARTIN LUTHER

Write a letter to Martin Luther to convince him to change his ideas and come back to the Catholic Church.

Note: Just encourage the child to write what he or she loves about the Catholic Church.

CRAFT PROJECT: BUILD A PAPER 3-D CASTLE

Materials:

☐ Scissors

☐ Glue

☐ Template from Activity Book *(Activity Book page 23)*

Instructions:

1. Color the template from the Activity Book.
2. Cut out template.
3. Glue template together to form your castle.
4. Enjoy!

DRAWING PROJECT: HIERARCHY OF FEUDAL SYSTEM

Materials:

☐ Paper

☐ Crayon

☐ Ruler

Instructions:

1. Using a ruler, draw a large triangle on the paper.
2. Horizontally divide the triangle into 4 sections.

3. Write the order of the feudal system beginning with *King* at the top, then *Nobles*, *Knights*, and *Peasants* at the bottom.
4. Color each section a different color.
5. Put a title at the top: *The Feudal System*.

CHAPTER 5
HENRY VIII AND ANGLICANISM

QUESTIONS FOR REVIEW:

1. **Why were the Lutherans known as "Protestants"?**
   They *protested* against the emperor, who wanted his entire realm to remain Catholic.

2. **Who was king of England in 1509, known as "Defender of the Faith"?**
   Henry VIII.

3. **After he became angry with the Church, what oath did King Henry force everyone to take?**
   To proclaim him the Supreme Head of the Church of England.

4. **Why was this wrong?**
   Only the pope is the head of the Church.

5. **What was the name of the new church created by King Henry?**
   The Anglican Church.

NARRATION EXERCISE:

King Henry VIII

Henry became king of England in 1509. He was married to Catherine, his brother's widow. Henry began as a good and devout king. He loved the Catholic faith. When he heard of Martin Luther, he wrote a book attacking Luther's heresies and eventually became known as "Defender of the Faith." But things were not well with King Henry. He fell in love with Anne Boleyn, even though he was already married. King Henry asked the pope for an annulment from Catherine so he could marry Anne. Pope Clement VII refused to grant him the annulment. This made Henry so angry that he started threatening the pope. As Henry moved closer to Anne, who was a Protestant, he grew angrier with the Church and started considering whether there were some advantages to Protestantism.

Henry decided that he wanted to be in control of the Church in England, forcing everyone to swear an oath to it. Once he did this, he sent Catherine away and married Anne instead. He had the old Catholic Mass thrown out and replaced by a service that was much more Protestant. This new Church Henry created was called the Anglican Church. The Anglican Church still exists today, and it is still governed by the monarch of England.

GAME: CHALLENGE GAME (2 PLAYERS)

Materials:

☐ Scissors

☐ Colored pencils

☐ Templates from Activity Book *(Activity Book pages 25-27)*

Instructions:

1. Cut out the pages for the game board, game pieces, and game cards.

2. Cut out and color the game pieces and game board.

3. Cut out the game cards and place them facedown in middle of board.

4. Player 1 draws a card but gives it to player 2, who will ask the question. If player 1 gets the answer right, proceed the number of spaces indicated on the card. If incorrectly answered, the player remains in that spot. Put used cards aside and reuse for the next round.

5. Repeat for player 2.

6. Winner is the first one to the end of the game board.

   *Encourage students to look for the answers in the book or ask for hints if they are having difficulty remembering.

CROSSWORD PUZZLE: HENRY VIII AND ANGLICANISM

(Activity Book page 29)

Answer Key:

Across:

   6. Germany

   7. Anglicanism

   8. Anne

Down:

   1. heresy

   2. Tower Hill

   3. Charles

   4. England

   5. convent

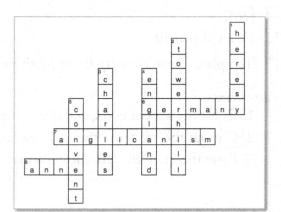

CRAFT PROJECT: SUGAR CUBE TOWER OF LONDON

Materials:

☐ Sugar cubes

☐ Frosting

☐ Plastic knife

☐ 10″ × 10″ cardboard base

☐ Foil

Instructions:

   1. Find a picture of the Tower of London.

   2. Wrap the cardboard base in foil.

   3. Apply frosting to the surface area of the cardboard where the model will be secured.

   4. Begin building a small scale tower out of sugar cubes, using frosting between each cube as you build.

CRAFT PROJECT: ST. THOMAS MORE CREST

Materials:

☐ Scissors

☐ Glue

☐ Colored pencils

☐ Templates from Activity Book *(Activity Book pages 31–33)*

Instructions:

1. Color the ax, the book, and the quote.

2. Cut out the crest and the ax, book, and quote.

3. Paste the ax on the left, the book on the right, and the quote on the bottom.

COLORING PAGE: THOMAS MORE

(Activity Book page 35)

Color the picture of Thomas More just before he becomes a martyr.

CHAPTER 6
THE FRENCH WARS OF RELIGION

QUESTIONS FOR REVIEW:

1. **What is the belief that God decides (predetermines) who will go to heaven and who will go to hell?**
   Predestination.

2. **Who believed in this belief (#1)?**
   John Calvin.

3. **What might happen to the people who challenged Calvin?**
   They could be executed.

4. **What were the wars between the supporters of Guise and Bourbon called?**
   The French Wars of Religion.

5. **Who supported the Duke of Guise and the Duke of Bourbon?**
   The Catholics supported Guise. The Huguenots supported Bourbon.

NARRATION EXERCISES:

John Calvin
John Calvin was a lawyer and a French Protestant. He taught that because of sin, mankind is totally and absolutely evil; so evil, in fact, that he cannot even turn to God. According to Calvin, God decides for all eternity who will go to heaven and who will go to hell; this belief is known as predestination. Calvin also taught that Jesus Christ did not die for all men but only for the righteous. People in France read Calvin's writings, and some adopted his views, helping contribute to the split in French society between the Huguenots and Catholics.

The French Wars of Religion
Queen Catherine did the best she could to help her son govern France. Supporters of Guise and Bourbon began fighting each other in 1562. This was the beginning

of the French Wars of Religion. The fighting was very nasty on both sides. For the next thirty-six years, Huguenots and Catholics would fight for control of the French throne. By 1593, Queen Catherine was dead, and the Bourbons were winning the war. The leader of the Bourbons, Henry of Navarre, would become king, although he was not Catholic. He finally decided to convert to Catholicism. According to legend, when he realized Paris would never accept him unless he converted, he shrugged and said, "Paris is worth a Mass."

WORD SEARCH: THE FRENCH WARS OF RELIGION

(Activity Book page 37)

Find these words from chapter 6.

Answer Key:

1. Catherine
2. Calvin
3. predestination
4. joust
5. Protestant
6. Reformation
7. Catholic
8. France
9. salvation
10. Nantes

```
E  M  B  F  T  G  S  S  I  S  R  G  C  N  C
C  J  B  R  F  P  A  K  A  E  L  T  O  L  A
N  J  O  U  S  T  R  L  P  V  S  I  A  K  T
A  X  F  V  S  E  V  O  D  E  T  O  F  G  H
R  E  P  B  F  A  V  S  T  A  M  B  O  Q  E
F  A  W  C  T  G  E  T  N  E  W  Q  I  U  R
L  H  O  I  O  T  R  I  B  B  S  V  B  U  I
L  K  O  M  N  F  T  M  T  I  J  T  A  E  N
N  N  A  A  J  S  C  I  L  O  H  T  A  C  E
Y  I  N  R  E  F  O  R  M  A  T  I  O  N  X
S  D  V  D  N  U  E  O  C  V  B  Z  S  O  T
K  T  E  L  J  V  D  E  H  U  I  P  M  H  C
U  R  N  F  A  T  U  K  X  H  R  O  O  M  C
P  N  B  W  M  C  X  I  D  V  S  V  B  V  L
S  Q  T  G  X  I  Z  Q  P  Y  J  B  X  J  H
```

DOUBLE PUZZLE: THE FRENCH WARS OF RELIGION

(Activity Book page 38)

Unscramble the words from the section "The French Wars of Religion." Copy the letters in the numbered blocks to the blocks with the corresponding numbers at the bottom to help answer the question.

Henry wondered how he could be king of France because he was a _____.

Answer Key:

Duke

Catherine

Henry

Guise

Bourbons

Navarre

Legend

Paris

Converted

Zealous

Huguenot

KUED	D U K E(5)
RAINEHCET	C A T H(1) E R I N E
NYRHE	H E N R Y
IUSEG	G(3) U I S E
BUOBONSR	B O U(2) R B O N S
RENRAAV	N A V A R R E
DENELG	L E G E N(6) D
SARPI	P A R I S
DOTVNERCE	C O(7) N V E R T(8) E D
LEAUZSO	Z E A L O U(4) S

SNACK PROJECT: QUEEN CATHERINE CROISSANTS

Materials and Ingredients:

☐ 1 tube of croissant dough

☐ Sandwich fillings of your desire (for example: ham and cheese, peanut butter and jelly, Nutella)

☐ 8 toothpicks

☐ Template of the French flag (3 mini flags)

☐ Scissors

☐ Colored pencils

☐ Tape

☐ Templates from Activity Book *(Activity Book page 39)*

Instructions:

1. Preheat oven and prepare the croissants as directed on package.
2. Cut out and color the mini French flags in Activity Book.
3. Tape the flag to a toothpick.
4. When croissants are complete, cut them open to make sandwiches of your liking.
5. Stick the French flags on top of each croissant sandwich.
6. Display, share, and enjoy!

CRAFT PROJECT: JOUSTING SWORD

Materials:

☐ Large roll of gray or silver duct tape

☐ Yardstick

☐ Dark-colored washcloth

Instructions:

1. Cover the yardstick with duct tape.
2. Form the tip of the sword at the end by using more duct tape.
3. Wrap the dark-colored washcloth around the other end of the yardstick for the handle.
4. Secure it with more duct tape.

CHAPTER 7
MARY, QUEEN OF SCOTS

QUESTIONS FOR REVIEW:

1. **Who became queen of Scotland after her father died?**
   Mary, daughter of James V.

2. **Who used to be a Catholic priest but wrote books that attacked the queen of Scotland?**
   John Knox.

3. **What was the queen forced to do while imprisoned?**
   She had to give up the throne (abdicate).

4. **What sad ending happened to the queen?**
   She was beheaded by her cousin Queen Elizabeth.

NARRATION EXERCISE:

Mary, Queen of Scots
The king of Scotland, James V, had only a little daughter, Mary, to succeed him on the throne. To keep her safe, he sent her to France. Later, Mary was wedded to the French prince. Then in 1559, her husband became king of France and she became queen. But eventually her father was killed in battle. Mary's husband then died, and she was no longer wanted in France. Mary returned to Scotland to assume the throne left empty by the death of her father. Many of the Scottish nobles did not want Mary to rule them. They had fallen under the influence of a preacher called John Knox, who hated Mary. After being attacked and defeated by the Lords of the Congregation, Queen Mary was imprisoned and forced to sign a document saying she abdicated the throne. But her captors felt sorry for her and helped her escape. She was able to raise an army and attack the Lords of the Congregation to get her throne back. She was defeated again and had to flee into England where her cousin Elizabeth ruled. Elizabeth saw Mary as a threat, locked her up, and eventually had her beheaded.

MAZE: MARY ESCAPES THE CASTLE PRISON

(Activity Book page 41)

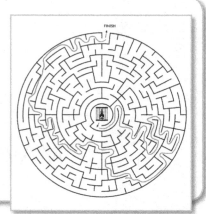

Instructions:
Help Mary escape from her captors and find freedom. Imagine how Queen Mary felt when those who captured her actually wanted to get her out of the prison. Help them escape to be finally free outside the walls of the castle.

WRITING ASSIGNMENT: A QUEEN'S SAD JOURNEY

(Activity Book page 42) Instructions:
Use the following events to write complete sentences about the things that happened to Queen Mary. The events are out of order. Decide the order of the events first and then create your sentences, writing them down in the correct order.

Answers (Should Be in Complete Sentences. Example Follows):
1. Queen Mary takes over as queen of Scotland.
2. Next, she is defeated and imprisoned by the Lords of the Congregation.
3. Then she is forced to give up the throne.
4. However, she is set free by her captors.
5. She flees south to England.
6. Finally, she is beheaded by her cousin.

CRAFT PROJECT: QUEEN MARY'S CROWN

Materials:

☐ Small assorted craft jewels (or cut-out small shapes from colored construction paper)

☐ Glue

☐ Colored pencils or crayons

☐ Tape

☐ Template from Activity Book *(Activity Book page 43)*

Instructions:
1. Cut out the template for the queen's crown in the Activity Book.
2. Color it as desired.
3. Decorate with assorted craft jewels.
4. Attach around head with tape.

CROSSWORD PUZZLE: TROUBLE ON THE WAY TO MASS

(Activity Book page 45)

Answer Key:

Across:

   4. abomination

   6. Edinburgh

   8. Royal Mile

Down:

   1. dawn

   2. scandal

   3. congregation

   5. Mamerot

   7. fruit

   9. Mary

COLORING PAGE: QUEEN MARY

(Activity Book page 47)

Color the picture of Queen Mary being prevented from going to Mass.

CHAPTER 8
THE COUNTER-REFORMATION

QUESTIONS FOR REVIEW:

1. **Which pope summoned the Council of Trent?**
    Pope Paul III.

2. **What three virtues did the Council of Trent say were necessary to go to heaven?**
    Faith, hope, and charity.

3. **St. Charles Borromeo is known to be the patron saint of what?**
    Bishops.

4. **What stopped Ignatius of Loyola from becoming a knight?**
    His leg was struck by a cannonball, leaving one leg shorter than the other, which caused him to limp.

5. **Who founded the religious order called the Society of Jesus, or the Jesuits?**
    St. Ignatius of Loyola.

NARRATION EXERCISE:

The Council of Trent
Pope Paul III summoned the Council of Trent in 1545, which had two purposes: first, to clarify Church teaching on things the Protestants attacked; second, to reform the life and morals of the clergy so that priests, bishops, and religious could be holier and set better examples for their people. The council taught that Catholics get their faith from the Bible *and* the Sacred Tradition of the Church. It also reaffirmed the ancient Christian belief that faith, hope, and charity were necessary to go to heaven and taught that indulgences, veneration of saints, and the use of images to worship were good and pious practices. Finally, the council also taught that the Body and Blood of Jesus Christ are truly present in the Eucharist and that faith, hope, and charity were necessary to get to heaven. As a result of the Council of Trent, the Catholic Church was reformed.

CRAFT PROJECT: PAPER BISHOP'S STAFF

Materials:

☐ Piece of white copier paper

☐ Scissors

☐ Tape

☐ Black pen

☐ Ruler

Instructions:

1. Cut an 8″ × 8″ square from the paper.

2. With one edge of the paper square facing you, decorate the opposite (top) edge with a single row of tiny crosses horizontally.

3. Do the same vertically on the right edge.

4. Flip the paper over so the crosses are now on the back.

5. Face a corner of the square toward you and begin rolling the paper into a tube until you reach the opposite corner. Try to keep it tight as you roll it.

6. Now you will need to tape the corner that is loose to the tube to keep it together.

7. Move your fingers about 6 inches up the tube, where you will pinch and flatten a small spot.

8. Then flatten and smooth out the next few inches of the tube.

9. Beginning at the end of the flat part, carefully roll the flattened section of paper around a pen or pencil until it is curly, like the end of a bishop's staff.

DOUBLE PUZZLE: THE COUNCIL OF TRENT

(Activity Book page 49)

Unscramble the words from the section "The Council of Trent." Copy the letters in the numbered blocks to the blocks with the corresponding numbers at the bottom to help answer the question.

This word describes the council.

Answer Key:

Council

Eucharist

Heaven

Faith

Hope

Charity

Reform

Morals

Ecumenical

WORD SEARCH: ST. IGNATIUS OF LOYOLA

(Activity Book page 50)

Find all the words related to St. Ignatius.

Answer Key:

1. Jesuits
2. Knight
3. cannon
4. limp
5. battlefield
6. education
7. priests
8. missionaries
9. Society of Jesus
10. service
11. saintly

GAME: FIND CHARLES BORROMEO'S MUSKET BALL

Materials:

☐ 1 marble

Instructions:

    1. Have one person hide the "musket ball" while the other one searches.

    2. When you've found it, yell out, "It's a miracle!"

    3. Repeat.

COLORING PAGE: AN ATTEMPTED ASSASSINATION

(Activity Book page 51)

    Color the picture of Charles Borromeo nearly being assassinated.

CHAPTER 9
POPE ST. PIUS V AND THE BATTLE OF LEPANTO

QUESTIONS FOR REVIEW:

1. **What did St. Teresa of Avila believe that nuns should focus on more?**
   Their spiritual life.

2. **Which friend of St. Teresa of Avila began reforming Carmelite monasteries?**
   St. John of the Cross.

3. **How did Pope Pius V respond to the threat of the Ottomans?**
   He created a navy, a Christian fleet.

4. **What did the pope ask all Catholics to do the night before the Battle of Lepanto?**
   Pray the rosary.

5. **What special feast is on October 7?**
   The Feast of Our Lady of the Rosary.

NARRATION EXERCISE:

The Return of the Turks

In 1570, the Turks invaded the island of Cyprus. The Christians of Cyprus fought bravely, but they were overwhelmed by the Turkish armies. When the island's capital was captured, the Turks murdered all the men—more than twenty thousand people—and sold the women and children as slaves. Before the island fell, the Venetians had asked the pope for aid. Pope Pius V was concerned about the threat of the Ottomans and wept for the Christians who had fallen under their rule. So he summoned all the Catholic kingdoms of Europe to donate men, ships, and supplies to build a mighty navy capable of defeating the Turks. The Christian alliance was called the Holy League and was led by John of Austria. They came upon the Turkish fleet near a place called Lepanto in the sea off the coast of

Greece. The Christian victory at Lepanto devastated the Turkish fleet and stopped the westward conquests of the Ottomans for more than a century.

MAP ACTIVITY: THE BATTLE OF LEPANTO

(Activity Book page 53) (see page 79 in your text book for help)

1. Shade the region (any color you like) showing the Ottoman Empire to see how big it was at the time of the Battle of Lepanto.

2. Find Sicily and draw a cross over it to show where the Christian Holy League departed from.

3. Find Lepanto near Greece, where the battle was fought. Draw two small ships, one to represent the Christian fleet and another to represent the Ottoman fleet.

4. Mark Rome with a cross in central Italy to show where the Ottomans had their sights set so they could conquer Christianity.

SNACK PROJECT: CHRISTIAN COOKIE SHIPS ON AN OCEAN OF JELL-O

Materials and Ingredients:

☐ Box of blue Jell-O

☐ Fruit leather cut into small triangle flags, about 1″ in length, one for each ship

☐ Clear glass baking dish

☐ 6–8 vanilla-, chocolate-, or strawberry-filled wafer cookies cut in half (these are the "ships")

☐ Toothpicks

☐ Scissors

Instructions:

1. Early in the day, prepare the Jell-O according to instructions and pour into a clear glass baking dish. Let set. This will be the ocean.

2. Pierce through each fruit leather "flag" with a toothpick.

3. Cut the wafer cookies in half, for a total of 12–16 cookie "ships."

4. Insert the toothpick flag into each ship.

5. Arrange the ships onto the blue Jell-O to show the Holy League's fleet sailing on the ocean.

GAME: BATTLE OF LEPANTO BATTLESHIP

Materials:

☐ Templates from Activity Book *(Activity Book pages 55-57)*

☐ Pencils

Instructions:

1. Cut out the two battleship game boards in the Activity Book, one for each player.

2. Two players face each other, not allowing the other team to see your game board.

3. Decide on 5–7 words you are going to use from the battle-scene story from chapter 9. Try not to use common words, but focus on words particular to this story. Words may cross at common letters (like a crossword puzzle).

4. Both players write their chosen words in the blank boxes, a letter in each box. You may decide to go vertically, horizontally, or diagonally (but always writing forward).

5. Once both players have their words in place, it is time to play.

6. Players take turns calling out coordinates. (A-6, G-10, etc.).

7. If it is a hit (meaning there is a letter in the box), the player who made the hit writes the letter on their "Opponent's Words" grid at the corresponding coordinates (opponent must call out the letter that was "hit"). If it was a miss, the player marks the box with an *X*.

8. Simultaneously, the opponent marks their grid. If it was a hit, the opponent circles the letter in the "My Words" grid box. If it was a miss, the opponent marks the box with an *X*.

9. If you guess a letter correctly, you get to go again until you miss.

10. Continue playing until you can either guess the word or the word is filled in with the correct letters.

11. When a word is guessed correctly or all letters of the word are guessed, say, "You sunk my ship."

12. Game is over when the first person guesses all the opponent's words.

COLORING PAGE: TWO GREAT SAINTS

(Activity Book page 59)

Color the picture of St. John of the Cross and St. Teresa of Avila.

CHAPTER 10
THE AGE OF ELIZABETH

QUESTIONS FOR REVIEW:

1. **Who was Mary Tudor's father?**
   King Henry VIII.

2. **Why didn't some of the nobles like Mary as queen?**
   She was Catholic.

3. **Who became queen after Mary Tudor died?**
   Her half sister, Elizabeth.

4. **Why did the pope excommunicate Elizabeth?**
   She was a false queen, and she had broken England away from the Church of Rome.

5. **What did Elizabeth do to make practicing Catholicism even harder?**
   She created the Penal Laws, which punished people for being Catholic.

NARRATION EXERCISE:

Queen Elizabeth and the Penal Laws
Elizabeth revived all the old laws from the time of Henry VIII and proclaimed herself Supreme Head of the Church of England. She again broke England away from the Church of Rome, outlawed the Mass, and compelled all her subjects to worship in the Protestant Anglican Church.

As a result, Pope St. Pius V excommunicated Elizabeth. He told English Catholics that she was a false queen and that they did not need to obey her. This obviously made Elizabeth much more hostile to Catholics. She created the Penal Laws, which punished Catholics for remaining loyal to the Church. These made it a crime to convert to Catholicism and even a crime to be a priest.

All English subjects had to attend Anglican services or pay a fine. Even so, there were many Catholics who continued to practice their faith in England despite the Penal Laws, and brave priests, at the risk of dying, came to England to minister to English Catholics in secret.

MAZE: HELP THE CATHOLIC PRIEST GET TO THE ALTAR TO SAY MASS

(Activity Book page 61)

Remember how the priests during the time of the Penal Laws had to find a way to say Mass in secret? They often had dangerous journeys and had to travel in disguise in order not to be recognized. Help Father make it to the altar unharmed!

CROSSWORD PUZZLE: MARY TUDOR

(Activity Book page 62)

Answer Key:

Across:

   2. Spain

   4. Henry

   7. Bloody Mary

   8. Cranmer

Down:

   1. Catherine

   3. Wyatt

   5. pope

   6. Edward

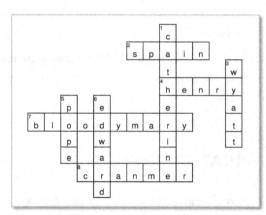

CRAFT PROJECT: PAPER ALTAR DIORAMA

Materials:

☐ Colored pencils

☐ Tape

☐ Scissors

☐ Glue stick

☐ Shoe box

☐ Template from Activity Book *(Activity Book pages 63-65)*

Instructions:

1. Color the template pieces (windows, chalice, and altar).
2. Cut them out. Fold and glue altar together.
3. Turn shoebox on its side and arrange and glue or tape template pieces to the surface of the shoebox.
4. Decorate the inside of the box with anything you want to make it look like a church.

CHAPTER 11
KING PHILIP II

QUESTIONS FOR REVIEW:

1. **Who was the king of Spain during the "Century of Gold"?**
   King Philip II.

2. **What was the king of Spain determined to do?**
   He was determined to stop the Protestant Reformation.

3. **Who got in the way of the king's plans?**
   Queen Elizabeth.

4. **What plans did the king make to attack England?**
   He launched the Spanish Armada.

5. **Who won the battle between the Spanish and the English?**
   The English.

NARRATION EXERCISE:

King Philip II
King Philip II was the son of Holy Roman Emperor Charles V. He inherited Spain from his father and reigned from 1556 to 1598. Philip built a palace called the Escorial, where he spent time praying and working long hours for the betterment of Spain. Philip, a serious Catholic, wanted to stop the Protestant Reformation from gaining any more ground in Europe. Philip did not get along well with England's new queen, Elizabeth, who wanted to be enemies with Spain. Philip and Elizabeth ended up fighting because of a region called the Low Countries. In the time of Philip II, many of the people of the Low Countries, especially in the Netherlands, had gone over to Protestantism. These people did not like being ruled by Philip. Soon, the Spanish were fighting the Protestants in a brutal war, which raged for years. Queen Elizabeth decided that she wanted to help the Protestant cause in the Netherlands. Philip began to make plans to attack

England, and he launched the Spanish Armada in 1588. Unfortunately, English ships were smaller and faster than the larger Spanish vessels, and only a precious few of the Spanish ships ever made it back to Spain. Philip died in the Escorial on September 13, 1598.

CRYPTOGRAM: A BATTLE FOR THE LOW COUNTRIES

(Activity Book page 67)

Read the section entitled "A Battle for the Low Countries" to answer what territories made up the Low Countries.

Answer: Netherlands, Belgium, Flanders, Luxembourg

CRAFT PROJECT: PAPER PLATE SPANISH ARMADA SHIP

Materials:

☐ Paper plate   ☐ Scissors

☐ Straws   ☐ Stapler

☐ Paper   ☐ Pencil

☐ Brown paints   ☐ Markers

☐ ½ of a paper towel roll   ☐ Hole punch

☐ Glue

Instructions:

For the Hull of the Ship:

1. Cut the paper plate in half.
2. Put the two halves together and cut straight across the bottom to make a straight edge.
3. Staple the two halves together in all four corners.
4. Decorate it with markers to make it look like a wooden ship (add windows, etc.).

For the Masts:

1. Cut out small strips of paper (the length of the straws and a bit wider) to resemble masts. Decorate with crosses.
2. Punch a hole in the top and bottom of each mast.
3. Insert the straws into each hole to assemble the masts.
4. Do this twice to make two masts.
5. Make and decorate triangular flags for the top of each mast. Attach with tape.

How to Insert Them Into the Ship:

1. Take the half of the paper towel roll and punch two holes on the top and a corresponding two holes on the bottom, one on the left and one on the right.
2. Insert the straw masks into the holes.
3. Place the roll of masts inside the paper plate ship, taping or gluing it so that it stays in place.

WORD SEARCH: KING PHILIP II

(Activity Book page 68)

Find all the words related to the Spanish king.

Answer Key:

1. Spain
2. England
3. Netherlands
4. Elizabeth
5. Philip

6. armada
7. Alba
8. sailors
9. Escorial
10. Europe

```
J X W S H T T S L A Y F L P A
U O S W T E S K S C S A O H B
E G X J E R D H J U X Z I L
S F M H B N X X V R S C A L A
M D I Y A R G T O Q D L U I X
K R N C Z D H C N N G F P H
T I W A I Y S J A M M I A S V
I U I H L E H A E N G L A N D
C C D J E R A K I W C C P P G
F D K L A R E X B L B Q R G S
J N V I M M I H E P O R U E L
W D U A W F P I T X M R S I B
V K D E Z W F H G E I F S L M
A A H G M B F D T L N R K L L
W K B X S H A F K U B U V F Y
```

CRAFT PROJECT: KING PHILIP II'S COAT OF ARMS

Materials:

☐ Scissors

☐ Glue

☐ Colored pencils

☐ Template from Activity Book *(Activity Book pages 69-71)*

Instructions:
1. Color then cut out the pieces you want for your coat of arms found in the Activity Book, or draw your own heraldic symbols!
2. Paste the symbols on the coat of arms.

CHAPTER 12
THE THIRTY YEARS' WAR

QUESTIONS FOR REVIEW:

1. **What order did King Ferdinand of Bohemia give to Protestant churches in 1617?**

   That Protestant churches on royal lands were to be closed and handed back over to the Catholics.

2. **When war eventually broke out in Bohemia between the Protestants and the Catholics, whom did the Protestants choose as their king?**

   A Calvinist named Frederick.

3. **What did thousands of Bohemian Protestants do after they were defeated in battle and their king Frederick fled?**

   They returned to the Catholic faith.

4. **Who then wanted to wage war against King Ferdinand and won many battles against the Catholics?**

   The Protestant king of Sweden, Gustavus Adolphus.

5. **What name is given to all of these wars fought throughout these years?**

   The Thirty Years' War.

NARRATION EXERCISE:

The Thirty Years' War

King Ferdinand had allowed the Protestants to maintain churches on private lands, but in 1617, he ordered Protestant churches on royal lands to be closed and handed back over to the Catholics. This enraged the Protestants of Bohemia. King Ferdinand and the Protestants began gathering armies for war. The Protestants chose Frederick as their king. Ferdinand, now the emperor, gathered Catholic armies from all over his empire and put them under the command of two men, Count Wallenstein and Count Tilly. They defeated the Bohemian Protestants and captured Prague. King Frederick fled. Ferdinand ordered Protestants to leave Bohemia or convert. Thousands of Bohemians returned to the Catholic faith. But the king of Denmark, Christian IV, was afraid of the growing power of Ferdinand and invaded Germany. Emperor Ferdinand won and had now defeated the Protestant Bohemians and the Protestant Danish. Unfortunately, the Protestant king of Sweden, Gustavus Adolphus, decided he wanted to try getting into the war against Ferdinand. Gustavus's army won battle after battle. Catholic armies could not stop him. More kingdoms got involved. It became very muddled who was fighting who and why. It was no longer a religious war but a war where each side was just trying to take land from the other. The Thirty Years' War ended with the Peace of Westphalia in 1648.

CROSSWORD PUZZLE: FERDINAND AND THE PROTESTANTS

(Activity Book page 73)

Read the section entitled "Ferdinand and the Protestants" to find the answers to the crossword puzzle.

Answer Key:

Across:

4. Bohemian

6. Wallenstein

7. armor

8. Adolphus

Down:

1. Frederick

2. volley

3. Matthias

5. faith

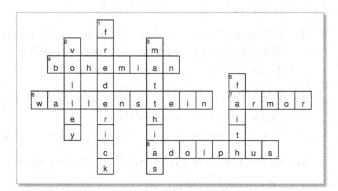

GAME: THE THIRTY YEARS' WAR

Materials:

☐ Plastic army soldiers (2 colors, 10–20 or more of each color)

☐ 4 small, bouncy rubber balls

Instructions:

1. Choose one color as the Catholics and another as the Protestants.
2. Each team sets up their soldiers on a hard floor or outside pavement.
3. Round one: Both teams stand behind their army and toss one ball toward the other army, trying to knock down as many soldiers as possible. Keep score by counting the number knocked down.
4. Round two: In this round, the first team goes alone first by tossing four balls at one time toward the other army. The second team does the same. Observe how each team might take out more of the opponent's soldiers at one time by using this "volleying" technique as King Adolphus did.

GAME: THE THIRTY YEARS' WAR CARD GAME

Materials:

☐ Deck of 52 cards

Objective: Be the first player to win all 52 cards.

Instructions:

1. Divide the deck evenly among two players, dealing the cards facedown.
2. Each player keeps his stack of twenty-six cards facedown.
3. Both players turn over a card at the same time. The player who has the highest card takes both cards and wins that small "battle." If both cards match, declare "war." Here, the players both turn a card facedown and one faceup. The player who has the high card showing gets all six cards. If the newly faceup cards are again the same, declare "war" again and repeat. Winner collects the whole pile.

CHAPTER 13
ROUNDHEADS AND CAVALIERS

QUESTIONS FOR REVIEW:

1. **Who became king of England in 1603?**
   King James VI of Scotland became King James I of England.

2. **Who tried to blow up Parliament because he was angry at the English government's treatment of Catholics?**
   Guy Fawkes.

3. **After the death of King James, who became king of England?**
   Charles Stuart, his son.

4. **What did King James and his son, King Charles, say about the relationship between the king and Parliament?**
   That a king is ruled by God's authority and did not have to answer to anyone else.

5. **Did Parliament agree with this?**
   No.

NARRATION EXERCISE:

King James, King Charles, and Parliament
King James VI of Scotland, the son of Mary, Queen of Scots, became King James I of England in 1603. He was king of both England *and* Scotland. King James did not get along well with the English Parliament, believing that a king ruled by God's authority alone and did not have to answer to anyone. When James died in 1625, his son, Charles Stuart, became king. Charles shared his father's poor view of Parliament. King Charles managed to rule for a long time without Parliament, coming up with all sorts of clever ways to get money without their consent. But eventually, he was forced to go to Parliament for money.

WORD SEARCH: ROUNDHEADS AND CAVALIERS

(Activity Book page 74)

Find all the words related to these two English factions.

Answer Key:

1. Parliament
2. Fawkes
3. James
4. Charles
5. gunpowder
6. England
7. Scotland
8. crown
9. Anglican
10. Puritans

```
I  J  K  Q  C  T  N  E  M  A  I  L  R  A  P
A  E  M  I  D  H  K  W  S  X  D  J  N  E  G
R  P  K  U  N  S  A  H  O  I  B  A  V  N  J
F  E  N  J  A  Z  Q  R  J  R  C  S  U  G  H
P  L  D  G  L  U  N  R  L  I  C  Z  U  L  F
Y  S  L  W  T  H  Z  T  L  E  X  F  L  A  W
K  L  V  A  O  I  Y  G  V  R  S  M  F  N  W
H  Y  H  R  C  P  N  X  T  Y  R  G  E  D  N
U  V  B  L  S  A  N  I  I  M  Q  O  F  L  R
O  V  W  Z  Y  S  P  U  R  I  T  A  N  S  I
P  P  Q  C  V  L  P  U  G  G  W  Y  E  F  S
M  V  Q  V  M  I  D  M  D  K  S  E  M  A  J
Q  M  W  B  W  X  N  S  E  N  K  S  E  C  E
G  I  S  I  C  E  G  S  U  T  I  O  O  N  A
Z  E  D  X  E  J  U  R  Z  Z  C  K  V  H  Q
```

DOUBLE PUZZLE: CROWN VERSUS PARLIAMENT

(Activity Book page 75)

Unscramble the words from the section "The Crown Versus Parliament." Copy the letters in the numbered blocks to the blocks with the corresponding numbers at the bottom to help answer the question.

Parliament was made up of what two chambers?

Answer Key:

Parliament

Nobility

Lawyers

Mayors

Elected

Laws

Tax

Kingdom

Authority

Roundheads

Cavaliers

TAMRENLAPI	P A R L I A M E N T
BYITILNO	N O B I L I T Y
RAYWELS	L A W Y E R S
SYRMOA	M A Y O R S
EEDECTL	E L E C T E D
SALW	L A W S
XAT	T A X
GOIKMND	K I N G D O M
TYITUROHA	A U T H O R I T Y
SORNUHDAED	R O U N D H E A D S
RACSIVEAL	C A V A L I E R S

House of Commons and House of Lords

SNACK PROJECT: GUY FAWKES GUNPOWDER COOKIES

Ingredients:

☐ Package of premade sugar cookie dough

☐ Can of premade frosting

☐ 2–3 packages of Pop Rocks

Instructions:

1. Prepare the cookies as instructed on the package. Let cook.
2. Frost the cookies.
3. Decorate with Pop Rocks.
4. Enjoy the explosion of flavor!

CHAPTER 14
THE RESTORATION AND THE NOT-SO-GLORIOUS REVOLUTION

QUESTIONS FOR REVIEW:

1. **Who invaded Ireland, causing a bitter and long war?**
   Oliver Cromwell.

2. **After the lord protector of England died, who eventually became king?**
   Charles II.

3. **What event forced the king to rebuild London?**
   The Great Fire of 1666.

4. **Who succeeded the king from question #2?**
   His brother James II.

5. **Who became king and queen of England after the king from question #4?**
   William and Mary.

NARRATION EXERCISES:

Oliver Cromwell

When Oliver Cromwell took control of Parliament, he declared England a republic and abolished the monarchy, making himself the single most powerful man in England. Cromwell's Parliament had King Charles condemned for treason against the English people and sentenced to death. Irish Catholics and English royalists attempted to gather forces to challenge Cromwell. The war was long and bitter, and Cromwell was ruthless. Cromwell outlawed the practice of Catholicism in Ireland, ordered priests to be murdered when captured, and took away most lands of the Catholic nobles and gave them to Protestants. Cromwell ruled as lord protector for nearly five years. His reign was a period of chaos, with constant uprisings against him.

King Charles II and the Return of the Monarchy

Cromwell fell ill and died in 1658. Parliament was soon restored, and they in turn wished to restore the monarchy. In 1660, Charles II was welcomed to London and hailed as king. As king, he quickly executed the men who had killed his father. After the restoration of the monarchy, Charles lashed out against Puritanism. Protestants who would not attend Anglican services were subjected to the same sorts of penalties as Catholics, and many Puritans fled England. Catholics did well under King Charles II because he liked them. But many of Charles's Protestant subjects were very unhappy with him; worst of all, he had no heir to the throne. Charles died in 1685. On his deathbed, he was received into the Catholic Church.

CRAFT PROJECT: WAX SEAL STAMP

Warning: Requires adult supervision

Materials:

☐ Hot glue gun and glue

☐ Air-dry clay

☐ 1 tack pin

☐ Craft paints

☐ Parchment paper

Instructions:

1. One day in advance, shape the air-dry clay into a seal stamp. Be sure to have one side flat.

2. On the flat side, use the tack pin to carve in your initials.

3. After a day, when your stamp is dry, you are ready to use it to make the wax seal.

4. Pour some glue gun wax onto parchment paper.

5. Using your stamp, make several seals into the glue. You should be able to see your initials.

6. Let it cool before touching.

7. After it is cool, peel off the seals and paint them if desired.

8. Use the seals on letters or envelopes.

MAZE: HELP THOMAS FARRINER AND HIS FAMILY FLEE THE FIRE!

(Activity Book page 76)

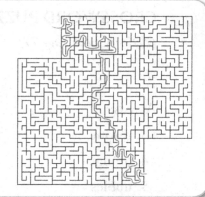

    Thomas Farriner and his family had to flee their home and run through the streets of London after the Great Fire of 1666 started spreading through the city. Help them get away from the fire and find safety.

GAME: PUT OUT THE GREAT FIRE OF 1666

Materials:

- ☐ Poster board
- ☐ Poster-board paints or poster markers
- ☐ Water balloons
- ☐ Scissors

Instructions:

1. On the poster board, draw, color, or paint large flames to resemble a fire.
2. When the poster is dry, cut out three holes large enough for a small water balloon to fit.
3. Fill several water balloons.
4. To play, one person holds up the poster of fire while another person attempts to toss balloons into the holes to put out the fire.

Caution: Participants may get wet!

CROSSWORD PUZZLE: THE GLORIOUS REVOLUTION

(Activity Book page 77)

Answer Key:

Across:

   3. throne

   4. orange

   5. nobles

   7. Stuarts

Down:

   1. Parliament

   2. nerve

   6. Mary

COLORING PAGE: ESCAPING THE GREAT FIRE

(Activity Book page 79)

Color the picture of Felicity and Mrs. Farriner running away from the fire that spread throughout London in 1666.

CHAPTER 15
THE AGE OF THE SUN KING

QUESTIONS FOR REVIEW:

1. **What other name was given to King Louis XIV because of the brilliance of his court at Versailles?**

   The Sun King.

2. **Which great theologian of the Church lived and worked during the time of Louis and is known as a champion of Marian veneration?**

   St. Louis de Montfort.

3. **In 1673, what extraordinarily important event took place in a convent of nuns in France?**

   Jesus appeared to St. Margaret Mary Alacoque.

4. **What did Jesus ask of St. Margaret Mary Alacoque?**

   To promote devotion to His Sacred Heart.

5. **How long was King Louis XIV's reign?**

   Seventy-two years.

NARRATION EXERCISES:

King Louis XIV

Louis XIV was born in 1638. When Louis was still young, he reigned with the help of a churchman, Cardinal Mazarin. Since Louis distrusted the nobles of France, and he did not want them to revolt again, he constructed a magnificent palace for himself at Versailles, where any noble who wanted to have the king's good opinion had to attend to him there. The nobles had to follow a strict code of etiquette, including what to wear and what to eat. Because of this, Louis made the nobles dependent upon him and incapable of resisting his power. King Louis XIV waged many wars to try to make France as powerful as possible. In 1685, he revoked the Edict of Nantes. The Catholic Church flourished under Louis. During his lifetime, there were many great saints and even martyrs among the Jesuits who went to North America.

St. Margaret Mary Alacoque
On December 27, 1673, Jesus Christ appeared to a young nun named St. Margaret Mary Alacoque. As she knelt in prayer before the Blessed Sacrament, her heart was flooded with warmth. All she could think about was the love of Jesus. With the eyes of her heart, she saw an image emerging in light. It was Jesus, bathed in a warm glow and coming toward her. Christ took Margaret Mary and placed her head upon his chest. When asked if she would give her heart to Christ, she replied, "Please take my heart, dear Lord!" In that moment in the vision, Jesus took her heart into his own hands and placed it within his Sacred Heart, prompting her heart to burst into flames. He would ask her to promote devotion to His Sacred Heart and for acts of reparation, for frequent Communion, Communion on the first Friday of the month, and the keeping of the Holy Hour.

CRAFT PROJECT: KING LOUIS'S WIG

Materials:

☐ Old baseball cap or painter's cap

☐ Glue
☐ Cotton

Instructions:
1. Glue cotton balls all over the outside of the cap, completely covering it.
2. After it dries, wear the cap backward so the brim is longer in the back, resembling King Louis's wig.

DRAMA PROJECT: THE SUN KING

Cast: King Louis XIV, Noble 1, Noble 2

Setting: In the Versailles Palace

Props: The wig from the craft project "King Louis's Wig"; small container with powder; table with chairs; couch/bed

The king sits in his palace, stroking his beard.

KING: Now that I have built my new palace in the countryside, I can get the nobles to be on my side, so they won't revolt like they did against my father.

Noble 1 knocks on door.

NOBLE 1: May I enter, your Majesty?

KING: Yes, please come in, dear sir, and make yourself at home. But you first must put on this wig.

NOBLE 1: Yes, your Highness.

King hands Noble 1 a wig, and he puts it on.
Noble 2 knocks on door.

NOBLE 2: May I enter, your Majesty?

KING: Yes, please come in, dear sir, but you must first powder your face.

NOBLE 2: Yes, your highness.

King hands Noble 2 some powder, and Noble 2
pretends to powder his face and coughs.

NOBLE 1: Just look at this place! So much to see and do! I am going to play poker!

NOBLE 2: I am going to waste my money too and eat a lot of food! I could spend all day and night here.

KING: Good to hear, good to hear! In fact, I have a table all ready for a feast. Join me.

NOBLE 1 AND 2 (TOGETHER): Thank you, your Majesty.

All sit down and pretend to eat.

KING TO NOBLE 1: Good sir, please do not slouch while dining!

KING TO NOBLE 2: And you may not put your elbows on the table!

NOBLE 1 AND 2 (TOGETHER): Yes, your Majesty.

KING: Now let us feast.

All continue pretending to eat. A moment later, the king yawns.

KING: Now that the feast is over, I need to go to sleep. You two go on and enjoy all the games I have for you to play.

Noble 1 and 2 arise and start to leave.

KING: Wait, not so fast, my good sirs! First, I need you to lay out my pajamas and turn down my bed.

NOBLE 1 WHISPERS TO NOBLE 2: Is he serious?

NOBLE 2 WHISPERS BACK: Better do as he commands. I mean, at least we get to have a night on the town for free.

Nobles 1 and 2 go to a couch or bed to pretend to
put out the king's pajamas and turn down the covers.
The king pretends to put on pajamas and gets in bed.

KING: Now you may proceed to the gaming hall. And bring more of your friends with you when you come tomorrow for more exquisite food and fun. The more nobles, the merrier!

NOBLE 1 AND 2 VERY EXCITEDLY: Yes, your Majesty! We will!

Nobles exit.

KING: Ah, yes! My plan is working! As long as the nobles keep coming to my glorious palace, they will never want to revolt against me again!

-THE END-

SNACK PROJECT: SACRED-HEART STRAWBERRIES

Materials and Ingredients:

- ☐ 12 strawberries
- ☐ Pineapple segments (canned or fresh)
- ☐ Chocolate frosting in a tube, small tip
- ☐ 24 toothpicks
- ☐ 12 mini marshmallows

Instructions:

1. Hull the strawberries and create a big enough opening to put in small pieces of pineapple segments. You will have to work with this to make sure exactly what size fits.
2. Put small pineapple segments into each hulled strawberry to resemble the fire of the Sacred Heart. If they don't stay in, don't panic. The toothpick crosses will hold them together.
3. Assemble "crosses" by putting two toothpicks together inserted through a small piece of marshmallow. The marshmallow should join the center of the crossbeams.
4. Insert the "cross" into the pineapple piece and in through the strawberry to hold it all together.
5. Pipe the frosting onto the front of each strawberry to resemble the crown of thorns.
6. Say a prayer to the Sacred Heart and enjoy!

COLORING PAGE: DEVOTION TO THE SACRED HEART

(Activity Book page 81)

Color the picture of St. Margaret Mary resting on Jesus's heart.

CHAPTER 16
THE TURKISH THREAT

QUESTIONS FOR REVIEW:

1. **What was the tax called that was put in place on Christians and non-Muslims, where Turkish officials would forcibly remove certain Christian boys between the ages of eight and eighteen from their homes?**
   The blood tax.

2. **What city were the Ottoman Turks planning to conquer around the mid-1600s?**
   Vienna.

3. **What country is this city (question #2) in?**
   Austria.

4. **Who won the siege at this city (question #2), the Ottomans or the Christians?**
   The Christians.

5. **Describe the Winged Hussars' armor.**
   The wings were wooden frames carrying eagle, ostrich, swan, or goose feathers. The Hussars wore heavy, plated armor and carried long, glistening spears that were razor sharp.

NARRATION EXERCISE:

The Siege of Vienna

By the mid-1600s, the Ottomans were preparing for another attempt to conquer the west. Their sights were set on the Austrian city of Vienna. If it could be taken, it would give the Turks a foothold from which to dominate central Europe. The Ottoman sultan, Mehmed IV, gathered a massive army to attack Vienna in 1683. The Holy Roman emperor, Leopold I, was desperate for help. He made an alliance with the king of Poland, Jan III Sobieski. He also allied with Venice and the Papal

States. Leopold and his allies began to gather their forces, but the Turks arrived at Vienna before the Poles did. Vienna was surrounded by 170,000 Turks who were working to knock down the city's walls. But then, the Polish army led by King Jan Sobieski arrived. Sobieski commanded 80,000 soldiers; a great number, but still much fewer than the Turks. But the Winged Hussars, Poland's cavalry, crashed into their enemies. Scores of Turkish soldiers were slain, and the rest turned to flee. After the battle, King Jan returned to the city to celebrate, saying, "I came. I saw. God conquered."

WORD SEARCH: THE TURKISH THREAT

(Activity Book page 83)

Find all the words that have to do with the Turkish threat.

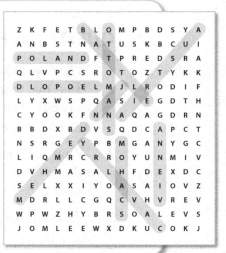

Answer Key:

1. Ottomans	6. Jan
2. Vienna	7. Poland
3. Austria	8. battle
4. Leopold	9. cavalry
5. Mehmed	10. Mohács

DOUBLE PUZZLE: THE BATTLE OF MOHÁCS

(Activity Book page 84)

Unscramble the words from the section "The Battles Continue." Copy the letters in the numbered blocks to the blocks with the corresponding numbers at the bottom to help answer the question.

Who was one of the heroes of the Battle of Mohács?

Answer Key:

Vienna	Exile
Hungary	Emperor Joseph
Turkish	Cavalry
Holy Roman Empire	Ottoman Empire
Crisis	**Eugene of Savoy**

NEIVAN	V I E N N A
RNHYUGA	H U N G A R Y
TIHSKUR	T U R K I S H
LYOH MANOR RIEMEP	H O L Y R O M A N E M P I R E
ISRISC	C R I S I S
LEXIE	E X I L E
REPREOM JEHPSO	E M P E R O R J O S E P H
VLCARYA	C A V A L R Y
TANTOMO MEPREI	O T T O M A N E M P I R E

CRAFT PROJECT: WINGED HUSSARS BROWN PAPER BAG PUPPET

Materials:

- ☐ Glue
- ☐ Scissors
- ☐ Colored pencils
- ☐ Standard-size brown paper lunch bags
- ☐ Red marker
- ☐ Templates from Activity Book *(Activity Book pages 85-89)*

Instructions:

1. Cut out the templates for Winged Hussar helmet and wings in Activity Book.
2. Color the helmet and wings with colored pencils (don't use markers; they will curl the paper).
3. Paste the helmet on the bottom side of the paper bag where it is closed.
4. Paste the wings behind that.
5. On the front of the paper bag, use the red marker to draw a large cross.
6. Put on a puppet show!

SNACK PROJECT: EDIBLE KNIGHT

Materials and Ingredients:

- ☐ Pringles
- ☐ Tostitos Scoops
- ☐ Mandarin orange slices
- ☐ Licorice
- ☐ Green peppers
- ☐ String cheese
- ☐ Knife
- ☐ Plate

Instructions:

1. Cut a piece of green pepper to look like a human torso or breastplate.
2. Cut the licorice to make arms, legs, a neck, and a belt.
3. Use one Tostitos Scoop for the head.
4. Place one Pringle at the end of one arm for the shield.
5. Place one string cheese at the end of the other arm for a sword.
6. Use a mandarin orange segment for the shoes.
7. Show your family, then enjoy!

COLORING PAGE: THE WINGED HUSSARS

(Activity Book page 91)
    Color the picture of the Polish fighter.

CHAPTER 17
THE JACOBITES

QUESTIONS FOR REVIEW:

1. **What does Jacobus mean?**
    James.

2. **What word means to leave one's country in order to settle in another?**
    Emigrate.

3. **What two countries became one under the name Great Britain?**
    Scotland and England.

4. **How did the British punish the Jacobites?**
    The Jacobites weren't allowed to wear traditional Scottish clothes or play Scottish music.

5. **What is a pretender?**
    Someone who claims to be a king or queen but is not recognized as a ruler.

NARRATION EXERCISE:

The Pretenders
After Queen Anne died in 1714, many Scots hoped Parliament would bring back the Stuarts. Instead, Parliament went to Germany and brought over a family called the Hanoverians. The first Hanoverian king, George I, could not even speak English. The British treated the Scots very harshly. By this time, King James II was dead, but his son, James Francis Edward Stuart, was alive and still claiming the throne. He was called the "Old Pretender" because he was claiming to be king but was not recognized as a ruler. Many Scottish Jacobites wanted the Old Pretender to rule, so they raised a rebellion in Scotland in his name, but in the end they were defeated. The Old Pretender saw the cause was lost and sailed away from Scotland. The Jacobites were not ready to give up. The Old Pretender had a son named Bonnie Prince Charlie, known as the Young Pretender. In April 1746,

Bonnie Prince Charlie and his Jacobite army chose to fight the British army under Duke William of Cumberland, the son of King George II, but were defeated. Bonnie Prince Charlie became a hunted man. He was able to stay hidden long enough to take a ship back to France.

MAZE: HELP THE SCOTS IMMIGRATE TO AMERICA

(Activity Book page 92)

Imagine how the Scottish people felt when they were forced from their homes. They chose to leave their country behind and go to America to find a happier life. Help them get there.

CROSSWORD PUZZLE: PUNISHING THE JACOBITES

(Activity Book page 93)

Answer Key:

Across:

  2. world

  6. rowdy

  7. Jacobite

  9. Stuarts

10. British

Down:

  1. clothes

  3. forts

  4. Charlie

  5. kings

  8. music

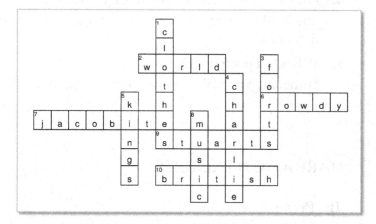

CRAFT PROJECT: FLOATABLE BOAT

Materials:

- ☐ 2 wine corks
- ☐ Toothpick
- ☐ Cereal box
- ☐ Hot glue gun
- ☐ Scissors
- ☐ Tape

Instructions:

1. Using the hot glue, connect the two corks side-by-side to form the floatable boat.
2. Let dry.
3. Cut out a small triangle from an old cereal box to make a decorative sail.
4. Tape the sail to the toothpick.
5. Insert the toothpick near the center of the two corks.
6. Float it!

WRITING ASSIGNMENT: MAKING A CONNECTION WITH THE SCOTS

Think of a time when you had to leave your home to go on a long trip. Or maybe you had to move into a new home, just like the Scots. Write about how you felt and what your experience was like as you left the comforts of your home and took a long journey to somewhere far away.

CHAPTER 18
LIGHT AND DARKNESS

QUESTIONS FOR REVIEW:

1. **During the Middle Ages, what invention made it easier for scientists and inventors to write about their discoveries?**
   The printing press.

2. **Who invented the telescope?**
   Galileo.

3. **What did William Harvey discover about the human heart?**
   How blood circulates through the body when the heart pumps.

4. **Whose laws are taught to those studying physics or math?**
   Sir Isaac Newton's.

5. **What fact about the sun did Nicolaus Copernicus discover?**
   That the sun, not the earth, is the center of the solar system.

NARRATION EXERCISE:

The Enlightenment
Some of the greatest changes in the 1600s and 1700s were how people thought about science. Due to the new knowledge gained during this period, it has been called the *Enlightenment*.

Many scientific discoveries were made. Some of them were medical, like when the Englishman William Harvey was the first to discover how the pumping of the heart circulates blood through the body. Other discoveries were technological, like the invention of the first microscope by the Dutch businessman Antonie van Leeuwenhoek. One of the most famous scientists was the English mathematician Sir Isaac Newton. He was interested in a variety of topics, including the study of light and the movement of planets. He was especially interested in how gravity worked. To this day, Newton's laws are taught to everybody who studies physics or math. Some scientists turned their gaze toward the heavens, like the Polish scientist and Catholic priest Nicolaus Copernicus. His study of the stars convinced him that the sun, not the earth, was the center of the solar system. Galileo was best known for the invention of the telescope, which allowed him to see marvelous things in space, such as sun spots and craters on the moon.

WORD SEARCH: THE ENLIGHTENMENT

(Activity Book page 94)
Find all the words that relate to the Enlightenment.

Answer Key:

1. Galileo
2. Copernicus
3. Newton
4. gravity
5. bacteria

6. academies
7. heart
8. Enlightenment
9. press

```
A M T M B H N G F H D I S T B
H C R F F E A X L N L P N A A
B J A S O L F P W P W E W Y C
E Z E D I B W Z A A M C I D T
F X H L E V Z J N Y L N F E
A V E Z E M J I E W L Y Q G R
N O O U S F I T G F D F W V I
G O C S C B H E A B Z Y Y X A
Z V T B J G E Q S U G W W P R
D M P W I C O P E R N I C U S
G X D L E A D B L Z T Y T S P
N Z N W K N R W J V V K E X A
H E H U Z W Q A W W Y R H O L
K M N B F H V G J Z P P Q O T
K D M Y G Q D Y T I V A R G T
```

CRYPTOGRAM: WHAT IS YOUR THEORY CALLED, GALILEO?

(Activity Book page 95)
After Galileo's experiment with the iron spheres, Enzo asked, "What is your theory called?"
"I'm thinking of calling it _____," Galileo answered.
Answer: THE LAW OF FREE FALL

CRAFT PROJECT: HOMEMADE TELESCOPE

Materials:

☐ Rubber band
☐ Tissue paper
☐ Empty cardboard paper towel roll
☐ Paint

☐ Paintbrushes
☐ Glue
☐ Confetti stars

Instructions:
1. Paint your paper towel roll any color.
2. Let it dry.
3. Cut a large piece of tissue paper big enough to cover and overlap the end of the paper towel roll.
4. Glue confetti stars to the piece of tissue paper.
5. Attach the tissue paper to the end of the paper towel roll using the rubber band.
6. Enjoy viewing the stars!

SNACK PROJECT: EDIBLE LEANING TOWER OF PISA

Materials and Ingredients:

☐ Recipe for Rice Krispies Treats

☐ Frosting

☐ Pie pan

☐ One wooden kitchen skewer (cut in half)

☐ White paper

☐ Toothpick

☐ Scissors

☐ Colored pencils

☐ Round cookie cutter

☐ Tape

Instructions:
1. Earlier in the day, prepare Rice Krispies Treats. Let set in a large jelly roll pan.
2. Prepare the flag by drawing a small flag on the paper. Color it green, white, and red, like the Italian flag.
3. Tape the flag to the toothpick. Set aside.
4. Using the round cookie cutter, cut out six to ten pieces of the Rice Krispies Treats.
5. In the pie pan, create the tower by stacking the pieces onto each other with a layer of frosting in between.
6. Gradually make it stand crooked.
7. To help it stand up, you can use the two kitchen skewers that were cut in half as a support by sticking them in the sides of the tower and extending to the base of the cake pan.
8. Insert the Italian flag on top and enjoy!

SCIENCE PROJECT: TESTING GRAVITY

Materials:

- ☐ Basketball
- ☐ Marble
- ☐ Baseball cap
- ☐ Large sofa cushion
- ☐ Paper clip
- ☐ Tennis shoe

Instructions:

1. Make a prediction as to which objects will hit the ground first if you dropped them all at the same time.
2. Take the basketball and marble.
3. Holding both, one in each hand at equal height from the ground (try to get high up, perhaps on a top bunk bed or over the stair railing), allow them to drop. Did you predict correctly?
4. Do the same with the baseball cap and the large sofa cushion.
5. Repeat with the paper clip and the tennis shoe.

COLORING PAGE: GALILEO

(Activity Book page 97)

Color the picture of Galileo just before he performs his experiment.

CHAPTER 19
A WORLD AT WAR

QUESTIONS FOR REVIEW:

1. **What is a piece of land under the control of another country called?**
   A colony.

2. **Where was the Seven Years' War fought?**
   All over the world.

3. **What was everyone mainly fighting for during this war?**
   Land.

4. **What caused King George III to agree to finally end the war?**
   The defeat at Yorktown by George Washington.

5. **What were some of the valuable materials supplied by the colonies?**
   Gold, spices, sugars, and silks.

NARRATION EXERCISES:

A Powerful Europe
The scientific advancements of the Enlightenment made Europeans the most advanced and powerful civilization on earth. For example, because of Newton's laws, military engineers were able to calculate precisely where a cannonball would strike based on the angle at which the cannon was fired. Because of this study of ballistics, their cannons became more accurate.

Another example is that all over the world, European explorers set up colonies, which supplied their mother countries with valuable materials, such as gold, spices, sugar, silks, and more.

These foreign lands did not always want European colonies there. Oftentimes the colonies were established by force. Most local people did not have strength to stand up to the Europeans, so huge chunks of the world began to fall under the control of Europe.

The Seven Years' War

In 1754, the French and the British got into a squabble over control of the Ohio Valley in North America. They both claimed the farming lands of Ohio, and neither side agreed to give them up. The war began when George Washington came across a French scouting party in the woods and attacked them. Soon, war broke out between France and Britain, and other countries joined. This war was called the Seven Years' War. The war was about land and plunder; *plunder* is the violent acquisition of property or other stolen goods. The war was fought all over the world. One of the war's decisive battles was the Battle of Quiberon Bay, where the British navy was victorious over the French.

MAP ACTIVITY: BATTLE OF QUIBERON BAY

(Activity Book page 99) (see page 178 in your text book for help).

1. Draw a small ship near the southern coast of Great Britain. Write "Royal George" somewhere on it, the name of the British ship from the story.

2. Draw another small ship off the west coast of France in the Quiberon Bay. Write "Superbe" on it, the name of the French ship from the story.

3. Draw a dotted path going south from your Royal George ship and around France to the Quiberon Bay to show the route the British ships took.

4. Write "November 20, 1759" where the two ships meet to signify the day this great battle took place.

DOUBLE PUZZLE: A REVOLUTION IS BORN

(Activity Book page 100)

Unscramble the words from the section "A Revolution Is Born." Copy the letters in the numbered blocks to the blocks with the corresponding numbers at the bottom to help answer the question.

What did Great Britain and the Americans sign to give independence to the United States?

Answer Key:

Yorktown

Great Britain

American

George Washington

Rebels

King George

Colonies

Taxation

Treaty of Paris

WYKNRTOO	Y O R K T O W N
GERTA NATBIRI	G R E A T B R I T A I N
CANMERAI	A M E R I C A N
GEGROE HONGATSWIN	G E O R G E W A S H I N G T O N
BRSEEL	R E B E L S
GINK GORGEE	K I N G G E O R G E
NEOCSLOI	C O L O N I E S
XOTNATIA	T A X A T I O N

CRAFT PROJECT: GEORGE WASHINGTON MASK

Materials:

☐ Scissors

☐ Tape

☐ Glue

☐ 2 craft sticks

☐ Cotton balls

☐ Markers

☐ Red, white, and blue construction paper

☐ Templates from Activity Book *(Activity Book page 101)*

Instructions:

1. Cut out the face and hat of George Washington from the Activity Book.
2. Trace the head of George Washington on the white construction paper.

3. Draw his eyes, nose, and mouth with marker (you may also wish to cut out the eyes for you to view through the mask). Cut it out.

4. Trace the hat on the blue construction paper. Cut it out.

5. Use the red construction paper to decorate the inside of the hat, giving it a border.

6. Tape the hat to the top of the face to create Washington wearing his hat.

7. Glue cotton balls around his face to give him the George Washington look.

8. Tape the two craft sticks together to make one long stick.

9. Tape the long craft stick to the back of George Washington.

10. You may enjoy this craft by acting out some of the scenes from "A Revolution Is Born."

GAME: BATTLE OF QUIBERON BAY BOWLING

Materials:

☐ 16 clothespins (the kind that you squeeze to open)

☐ Colored pencils

☐ Scissors

☐ Small, bouncy rubber ball

☐ Templates from Activity Book *(Activity Book page 103)*

Instructions:

1. Cut out the French and British soldier templates located in the Activity Book.

2. Color the French soldiers' hats blue and the British soldiers' hats red.

3. Attach the heads to the clothespins to create two teams.

4. Set up the two teams in any formation six to ten feet across from one another.

5. Decide which team to be on and who goes first.

6. Play the game by rolling the bouncy rubber ball toward the other team, trying to knock down as many soldiers as possible. If you miss, the other team gets a turn.

7. Remove any knocked-over soldiers and set them aside.

8. Continue playing until one of the teams is completely knocked over.

CHAPTER 20
THE FRENCH REVOLUTION

QUESTIONS FOR REVIEW:

1. **Who was the French king at the time of the American Revolution, and who was his wife?**
   King Louis XVI and Marie Antoinette.

2. **Which revolutionaries wanted to get rid of both the monarchy and Christianity?**
   The Jacobins.

3. **Whom did Robespierre execute during the Reign of Terror?**
   He executed about forty thousand French people, including priests, nuns, Catholics, and anyone loyal to the monarchy.

4. **What happened to the sixteen nuns of the Carmelite convent of Compiègne?**
   They were all beheaded.

5. **Who became the hero of the revolution when he loaded cannons full of small balls of metal and fired them into a mob of royalists?**
   Napoleon Bonaparte.

NARRATION EXERCISE:

Taking Down the Church
The National Assembly wanted to break the Catholic Church's influence in France and so began to nationalize all Church property—that is, to put the government in control of it. Monasteries and convents were also closed, and clergy were ordered to swear an oath of loyalty to the state. They even tried to create a new calendar so people would not go by the Church calendar anymore. There were radical revolutionaries called Jacobins who wanted to get rid of both the monarchy and Christianity altogether. The Jacobins took over the government of France, abolishing the monarchy and proclaiming France a republic. The Committee of

Public Safety, ruled by Maximilien Robespierre, executed around forty thousand French people during the Reign of Terror from 1793 to 1794. Most of all, Robespierre had a special hatred for the Catholic Church. In a place called the Vendée, Catholics were ruthlessly slaughtered by the troops of the republic. In other places, even priests and religious were victims of the guillotine.

WRITING ASSIGNMENT: ACROSTIC POEM

The nuns who were ruthlessly slaughtered during the Reign of Terror became martyrs of the Faith. Write an acrostic poem that describes their courage while facing death.

First, write the words "Song at the Scaffold" vertically on a sheet of paper. Then beginning with the letter *S*, write a phrase to describe the nuns that includes the letter *S* anywhere within the phrase. For example, you might write, "The nuns were meek" on the first line where the *S* is. Continue to do this until each letter is used. Notice that the phrase does not need to begin with the letter, but it can if you wish.

CROSSWORD PUZZLE: THE RISE OF NAPOLEON

(Activity Book page 105)

Answer Key:

Across:

  2. France

  5. Italy

  7. directory

Down:

  1. five

  3. royalists

  4. Napoleon

  6. hero

CRAFT PROJECT: CRAFT STICK CRUCIFIX

Materials:

- ☐ Colored pencils
- ☐ Scissors
- ☐ Glue
- ☐ 2 craft sticks
- ☐ Template from Activity Book *(Activity Book page 107)*

Instructions:

1. Color and cut out the template of the crucified Lord from the Activity Book.
2. Glue two craft sticks together at the center to form a cross.
3. Take the picture of the crucified Lord and glue it onto the craft sticks.

CRAFT PROJECT: CANNON MARSHMALLOW SHOOTER

Materials:

- ☐ Scissors
- ☐ Sturdy single-serve yogurt cup
- ☐ Balloon
- ☐ Mini marshmallows

Instructions:

1. Cut out the bottom of the yogurt cup.
2. Tie a knot at the end of the balloon where you normally would if it were blown up.
3. Cut off ½" from the bottom of the balloon.
4. Stretch the balloon over the larger end of the yogurt cup.
5. Insert marshmallows and shoot them out by pulling the end of the balloon.

CHAPTER 21
THE RISE AND FALL OF NAPOLEON

QUESTIONS FOR REVIEW:

1. **What is it called when someone overthrows a government leader and replaces him or her with someone else?**
   A coup.

2. **Who made himself the head of the government in France?**
   Napoleon.

3. **Where did Napoleon's army fight the British, only to be defeated?**
   Waterloo.

4. **What was the name of Napoleon's wife?**
   Josephine.

5. **How did the French soldiers fight during Napoleon's time?**
   They fought in large squares, some shooting while kneeling and others while standing.

NARRATION EXERCISE:

Napoleon Bonaparte
Napoleon led the French army in many battles, and for years nobody could stand up to him. He conquered Spain, and his armies defeated the Austrians. He swept away the Holy Roman Empire and beat the armies of Prussia. Napoleon wanted to restore relations with the Catholic Church. He and Pope Pius VII signed a concordat, which is an agreement between the Catholic Church and the government of a nation that lays down guidelines for how the Church and the government would interact. Napoleon wanted the pope to support him politically, but Pius refused. In 1809, he took the Papal States away from Pius and occupied Rome. Pius responded by excommunicating Napoleon. Napoleon then had Pius VII arrested. All of Europe was under Napoleon's power. After his plan to

defeat the Russian army failed, he sneaked away and rode home to France. He abdicated his throne and was exiled but soon escaped. Then thousands of men flocked to Napoleon, begging to fight for him. A combined army of British and Prussians under the Duke of Wellington marched out to meet Napoleon at a place called Waterloo, where he was defeated. He was exiled again, fell ill, and died on May 5, 1821.

MAP ACTIVITY: NAPOLEON'S CONQUESTS

(Activity Book page 109)

1. In the upper right corner of your map, write "1802–1815" to show the stretch of time Napoleon set out on his conquests of Europe.

2. Below that, write "1812." This is the year during which the French Empire was roughly at its height.

3. Color the following countries blue to show the extent of the French Empire at its height. Napoleon conquered all or at least most of these countries: France, Italy, Corsica, Spain, Germany, Netherlands, Belgium, Luxembourg, Croatia, Slovenia, Switzerland, Austria, and Poland.

   All these nations may not have had their current names or sovereignties at this time, but this will show you the extent of how big his empire was.

4. Color Russia red to show how the Russians withstood Napoleon's forces and sent him retreating, which began his downfall.

5. Find the dot in Belgium and write "Waterloo" next to it. This is where Napoleon met his demise.

CRAFT PROJECT: NAPOLEON'S HAT

Materials:

☐ 2 pieces of black felt, 18" long each

☐ Scissors

☐ Tape

☐ Craft glue

☐ Template from Activity Book *(Activity Book page 111)*

Instructions:

1. Cut out the template for Napoleon's hat in the Activity Book.
2. Fold your black felt in half and tape your template to the felt with the dotted line on the folded edge.
3. Cut the felt out around the hat template, leave the folded edge uncut.
4. Repeat steps 1-3 for the back part of your hat.
5. Measure for size by holding the pieces around the head of the child who will be wearing the hat; glue pieces together accordingly

SNACK PROJECT: NAPOLEON SANDWICH COOKIES

Ingredients:

☐ Graham crackers

☐ Whipped cream

☐ Strawberries

Instructions:

1. Slice up the strawberries into thin slices or pieces.
2. Begin by putting down a layer of whipped cream on one graham cracker.
3. Place a single layer of the strawberry slices on top of that.
4. Top that off with another graham cracker, pushing down a little to make a "sandwich."
5. Repeat this process until you have several layers of "sandwiches" on top of each other.
6. Enjoy!

WORD SEARCH: THE RISE AND FALL OF NAPOLEON

(Activity Book page 113)

Find all the words related to the French leader.

Answer Key:

1. Napoleon
2. Josephine
3. Waterloo
4. French
5. British
6. St. Helena
7. coup
8. monarchy
9. Pius

COLORING PAGE: NAPOLEON BONAPARTE

(Activity Book page 115)

Color the illustration of the famous French leader.

CHAPTER 22
PEACE RETURNS

QUESTIONS FOR REVIEW:

1. **Which saint is known as the Curé of Ars?**
    St. John Vianney.

2. **Besides the miracles performed by St. John Vianney, what was one of the most important things he did?**
    He brought many back to the faith by spending long hours in the confessional.

3. **St. John Vianney is the patron saint of whom?**
    Parish priests.

4. **What is the French word for "pastor"?**
    Curé.

5. **What word is given for those who want to keep things the way they are and prevent change from happening too much?**
    Conservatism.

NARRATION EXERCISE:

St. John Vianney
St. John Vianney was pastor of the parish church of Ars in France. He is known as the Curé of Ars. St. John was born during the French Revolution. As a boy, his family had to attend Masses said in barns by priests hiding from the government. During the time of Napoleon, St. John joined the seminary. He was ordained the year of Waterloo. He was not a very educated man, and many thought him dumb. But he was incredibly saintly and cared deeply about the souls of his congregation. He preached on holy living and spent more than twelve hours a day hearing confessions. He also led by example through his virtuous life and was a noted miracle worker. Many miracles would be attributed to him before his death

in 1859, but one of the most important things he did was spend all that time in the confessional, as it brought many back into the faith through Christ's mercy. He is the patron saint of parish priests.

DOUBLE PUZZLE: ST. JOHN VIANNEY

(Activity Book page 117)

Unscramble the words from the section "St. John Vianney." Copy the letters in the numbered blocks to the blocks with the corresponding numbers at the bottom to answer the question.

What is another name for St. John Vianney?

Answer Key:

Latin

Confession

Mass

John

Miracle

Orphanage

Vienna

Waterloo

Curé of Ars

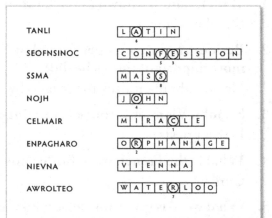

TANLI — L A T I N

SEOFNSINOC — C O N F E S S I O N

SSMA — M A S S

NOJH — J O H N

CELMAIR — M I R A C L E

ENPAGHARO — O R P H A N A G E

NIEVNA — V I E N N A

AWROLTEO — W A T E R L O O

WRITING ASSIGNMENT: MIRACLE OF THE GRAIN HAIKU

Write a haiku poem about the miracle that John Vianney performed at the orphanage.

Haiku is a poem that has exactly three lines. The first line has five syllables, the second line has seven syllables, and the third line has five syllables. It does not have to rhyme. Your haiku will be a simple summary of the miracle that happened in any way you want to express it. When you are finished, draw an illustration at the bottom of the poem.

SNACK PROJECT: ORPHANAGE OAT-AND-FRUIT BOWL

Ingredients:

☐ 1 cup of vanilla yogurt

☐ 1 crunchy granola bar

☐ Blueberries

☐ Raspberries

Instructions:

1. Place the yogurt into a small cup or coffee mug.

2. Mix some blueberries and raspberries into the yogurt.

3. Crumble the granola bar while still in the package.

4. Sprinkle the granola bar crumbs over the yogurt.

5. Enjoy!

COLORING PAGE: ST. JOHN VIANNEY

(Activity Book page 119)

Color the picture of the patron saint of priests.

CHAPTER 23
REFORMS AND REVOLUTIONS

QUESTIONS FOR REVIEW:

1. **What type of government involves the practice of people electing others (officials) to represent them and run the country or nation?**
   Democratic.

2. **What word is from the word *liberty*, which was a slogan of the French and American revolutions?**
   Liberals.

3. **What did the Reform Bill give to the common people?**
   The right to vote.

4. **Who was the Citizen King?**
   King Louis-Philippe.

5. **Which relative of Napoleon became the new emperor of France?**
   His nephew, Louis-Napoleon.

NARRATION EXERCISE:

The Citizen King
The new king of France, Louis XVIII, found the kingdom very divided. Louis died in 1824 and was succeeded by his younger brother King Charles X. He offended liberals and conservatives by refusing to listen to the advice of his counselors. Many in his government asked him to step down, but the king refused. The people of Paris rioted, and King Charles fled. The French throne went to Louis-Philippe, who thought he could work with the liberals. He tried to dress and act like a commoner and liked being called "the Citizen King." Louis-Philippe gave French liberals a constitution, which gave more Frenchmen the right to vote and granted more freedom of speech. But it also declared that Catholicism was no longer the official religion of France. Even though Louis-Philippe tried to be

popular with the people, they did not like him. Newspapers published insulting drawings of him. In 1848, the economy of France was in very bad shape. People started rioting to show their frustration. King Louis-Philippe was understandably afraid. He put on traveling clothes and, calling himself "Mr. Smith," ran off to England. That was the end of the Citizen King's reign.

CROSSWORD PUZZLE: REFORMS AND REVOLUTIONS

(Activity Book page 121)

Answer Key:

Across:

1. **grain**

3. **Smith**

7. **democratic**

8. **citizen**

Down:

2. **reform**

4. **monarchy**

5. **nephew**

6. **riots**

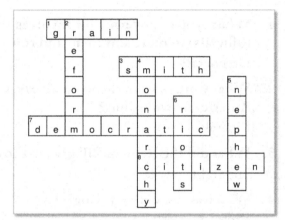

CRAFT PROJECT: THE REFORM BILL SCROLL

Materials:

- ☐ Large brown paper bag
- ☐ Markers
- ☐ Ruler
- ☐ String
- ☐ Scissors
- ☐ 2 unsharpened pencils
- ☐ Tape

Instructions:

1. Measure an 8 ½″ × 11″ rectangle onto a blank section of the paper bag.
2. Using your hands, carefully tear it out along the lines. It is OK if it does not end up the size you measured. Try to keep it rectangular.
3. Write the words "The Reform Bill" at the top center of the paper.
4. Recall some of the things from the chapter that the Reform Bill did and make a list on the paper.
5. Tightly crumble the paper into a wad with your hands.
6. Open it back up and continually smooth it out to make it flat. Repeat if needed.
7. Roll the Reform Bill into a scroll.
8. Tape two unsharpened pencils together to create one long one.
9. Insert the new long pencil into the center of the scroll to easily roll and unroll the document.
10. Cut a piece of string to tie the scroll together, but do not make a knot.

SNACK PROJECT: EDIBLE CORN LAWS

Materials and Ingredients:

☐ Write-on piping frosting (any color but white)

☐ Paper plate

☐ Popcorn (already popped)

Instructions:

1. On the paper plate, print out the words *The Corn Laws* to fit on the entire plate.
2. Place pieces of popcorn on top of the words.
3. Enjoy!

CHAPTER 24
THE UNIFICATION OF ITALY AND GERMANY

QUESTIONS FOR REVIEW:

1. **What word means "owning things in common"?**
   Communism.

2. **What is an atheist?**
   Someone who does not believe God exists.

3. **What were the cables called that allowed electronic messages to be sent?**
   Telegraph lines.

4. **What country declared war on Prussia in 1870 but was defeated?**
   France.

5. **What did Pope Pius IX publish in 1870?**
   A letter condemning the new Italian government and exposing all the evils that had happened to the Church in Italy.

NARRATION EXERCISE:

The *Communist Manifesto*

Two German philosophers named Karl Marx and Friedrich Engels published a book called the *Communist Manifesto*. They believed the problems in the world were due to the fact that the rich were always oppressing the poor and that the poor workers of the world should all unite and overthrow the rich. They also said all private property, whether of individuals or of the Church, should be taken away. There would be no more rich or poor. Mankind would be one single community, which is why it was called Communism. The Communists wanted to build their society through violent revolution and were thus enemies of nobles, kings, and queens, and especially of the Church and of religion in general. In their future society, Marx and Engels imagined there would be no more religion. Communism was just one of many ideas going around in those days about how to organize society.

DOUBLE PUZZLE: PRUSSIA

(Activity Book page 122)

Unscramble the words from the section on Prussia. Copy the letters in the numbered blocks to the blocks with the corresponding numbers at the bottom to help answer the question.

What two inventions did the Prussians make use of during the battles?

Answer Key:

Prussia

Wilhelm

Otto von Bismarck

France

German

Chancellor

Kaiser

Exile

Sedan

Railroads and telegraph lines

SIPASRU	P R U S S I A (19 9 22 10)
HILMEWL	W I L H E L M (3 20 24)
TOTO OVN RIACSKMB	O T T O (6 12) V O N (23) B I S M A R C K
CERAFN	F R A N C E (7 11)
MERNGA	G E R M A N (16 1)
COAREHLLNC	C H A N C E L L O R (4 14 17)
SERKIA	K A I S E R (18 25 5)
LEEXI	E X I L E (15 21 13)
DASNE	S E D A N (8 2)

CRAFT PROJECT: MORSE CODE MESSAGE

Materials:

☐ Paper

☐ Pens

☐ Template from Activity Book *(Activity Book page 123)*

Instructions:

1. Use the Morse code alphabet to write a short message to a friend, using only dots and dashes.

2. Have him or her do the same for you.

3. Translate each other's letters.

GAME: MORSE CODE GAME

Materials:

- ☐ Flashlight
- ☐ Paper
- ☐ Pencil
- ☐ Template from Activity Book *(Activity Book page 125)*

Instructions:

1. Think of a short word to communicate to your partner, like "hello."
2. Use the flashlight as Morse code by clicking it on and off quickly for dots and holding it on longer for dashes. Spell out the word with the Morse code to your partner.
3. The partner writes down the letters on paper until he figures out your word.

SNACK PROJECT: EDIBLE RAILROAD

Materials and Ingredients:

- ☐ Graham crackers
- ☐ Canned frosting
- ☐ Black licorice ropes
- ☐ 2´ × 2´ cardboard (size may vary)
- ☐ Foil

Instructions:

1. Cover the large cardboard with foil. This will be used as a base upon which to construct your railroad.
2. Carefully break the graham cracker squares into halves. These are the railroad ties.
3. Lay out the railroad ties around the cardboard base to begin constructing your railroad. Use a combination of straight and curved lines going all around the cardboard.
4. Once you decide what it will look like, "glue" the ties down with frosting on the bottom.
5. Put a small dollop of frosting on the corners of each tie that is now glued down.
6. Place the licorice ropes on top of each dollop to secure the "rails."
7. Continue constructing the "rail" onto each "tie" until your railroad is complete.

COLORING PAGE: NAPOLEON III'S SURRENDER

(Activity Book page 127)

Color the picture of Napoleon III surrendering to Otto von Bismarck, a minister in the kingdom of Prussia.

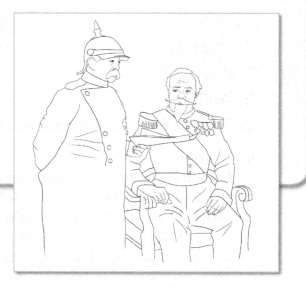

CHAPTER 25
THE POPES AGAINST THE WORLD

QUESTIONS FOR REVIEW:

1. **What did Pope Pius IX refuse to do for the rest of his life because he thought Italy was behaving so wickedly?**
   He refused to leave the Vatican.

2. **What were the popes called who did the same thing for almost sixty years?**
   "Prisoners of the Vatican."

3. **What does *infallible* mean?**
   Not capable of being wrong on matters of faith and morals.

4. **What prayer that is often prayed at the end of Mass was written by Pope Leo?**
   The prayer to St. Michael.

5. **Who made all new priests swear an oath against Modernism?**
   Pope Pius X.

NARRATION EXERCISES:

Pope Pius IX
Pope Pius IX opposed the Kingdom of Italy because it was very anti-Catholic and the government shut down monasteries and convents. Many church lands were confiscated, and laws were passed making it difficult to send children to religious schools. Pope Pius IX thought the Kingdom of Italy was behaving wickedly, so he refused to leave Vatican City. For the rest of his life, he never left the Vatican, and future popes did the same. He defended the Church by summoning the First Vatican Council in 1870, which taught that the pope is infallible when he teaches officially on matters of faith and morals. The Catholic Church had always believed this. But with all the attacks on the Church's authority, Pius IX thought it was the right time to declare this to the world.

Modernism

Some priests and theologians began applying the idea of change to Catholicism. These people taught that Christians should stop believing in miracles, that Jesus never rose from the dead, that the Bible was not true, and many other damaging things. They believed that since modern man had developed, so must God. St. Pius X called these people "Modernists" and said they were teaching heresy. He took strong action against the Modernists. He forbade them from teaching in seminaries and religious schools, discouraged Catholic publishers from publishing Modernist writings, and refused to promote them to important Church offices. He also made all new priests swear an oath against Modernism.

WORD SEARCH: POPE PIUS IX

(Activity Book page 129)

Find the words that relate to Pope Pius IX.

Answer Key:

1. troops

2. Catholic

3. lands

4. Vatican

5. pope

6. priest

7. republic

8. council

9. infallible

```
S M T G C F S X N P D F R D F
E Q O M A S G I B I Y E R U A
B V F H T P E P D M P G F I J
J P G M H O V G O U S I U E S
I B O B O O S I B P D L K F A
M N L S L R B L B S E D Z S S
F Q F K I T I E L X Y W W T V
X V S A C C N A C I T A V N J
V R C S L W R E R S C B G X C
Z A J L T L L B E Y Z N X M L
L C K H H Q I I Z Q M R U G U
J H A Z O O R B L A N D S O T
G F G Z U P F R L R F Z R A C
I G A O F J Y K E E K A P M D
G C V R F S L R Z I E V P M B
```

CRAFT PROJECT: PRAYER TO ST. MICHAEL SHIELD

Materials:

- ☐ White poster board
- ☐ Pencil
- ☐ Markers (various colors)
- ☐ Scissors
- ☐ Ruler

Instructions:

1. Draw a large shield on the poster board with the pencil.
2. Outline the shield with a marker.
3. Cut out the shield.
4. Use the ruler to draw horizontal lines on the shield. This is where you will write the prayer.
5. Write the prayer to St. Michael on the lines you made on the shield (you can find it in your Text Book in chapter 25).
6. Decorate the shield with swords and crosses.

CRAFT PROJECT: SWISS PONTIFICAL GUARD DRUM

Materials:

- ☐ Container (such as an oatmeal or ice cream tub)
- ☐ Yarn
- ☐ Packing tape
- ☐ Chopsticks
- ☐ Craft foam
- ☐ Markers
- ☐ Butcher paper
- ☐ Scissors
- ☐ Ruler

Instructions:

1. Smoothly cover the top of the container with packing tape to make the top of the drum. Do two or three sturdy layers that overlap the container. Make sure it is tight.

2. Decorate the outside of the drum with butcher paper. Use markers to draw crosses on the drum.

3. Poke two holes on two sides of the container.

4. Put a long piece of yarn through the holes that is long enough to go around your neck so that the drum is hanging at your waist. Tie the yarn.

5. For the drumsticks, cut out two long, skinny strips of craft foam (about 6–8″ in length).

6. Tape one end of the craft foam to one of the chopsticks.

7. Tightly roll the foam around the top of the chopstick to form the top of the mallet.

8. Secure it with more tape around the top of the chopstick.

9. Repeat steps 5–8 to make a second drumstick.

10. Your drum is complete and ready to play!

CRAFT PROJECT: ST. MICHAEL'S FLAMING SWORD

Materials:

- ☐ Orange and red markers
- ☐ Tape
- ☐ A wooden yardstick
- ☐ A 6″ or 12″ wooden ruler
- ☐ Duct tape
- ☐ Glue
- ☐ Scissors
- ☐ Template from Activity Book *(Activity Book pages 131–133)*

Instructions:

1. Cover the yardstick completely with duct tape.
2. Cover the ruler completely with duct tape.
3. Attach the ruler to one end of the yardstick to make the handle for the sword.
4. Color and cut out the flames from the Activity Book.
5. Glue or tape the flames along both sides of the yardstick, flame side outward, beginning at the top and ending three-quarters of the way down.
6. Your sword is ready for battle!

COLORING PAGE: PENNING THE PRAYER TO ST. MICHAEL

(Activity Book page 135)

Color the picture of Pope Leo XIII writing down his prayer to St. Michael, with the archangel sitting over his shoulder.

CHAPTER 26
EUROPE CONQUERS THE GLOBE

QUESTIONS FOR REVIEW:

1. **The Chinese who attacked Europeans living in China called themselves "Fists of Righteousness," but what name did the British give them?**
    Boxers.

2. **What countries eventually defeated this group?**
    France, Germany, Britain, and America.

3. **During the Sepoy Mutiny, who also attacked the British?**
    The Indians.

4. **What are some positive things about European colonization?**
    They brought electricity, railroads, hospitals, and Christianity wherever they went.

5. **In 1857, there was a massive revolt against British rule called what?**
    The Sepoy Mutiny.

NARRATION EXERCISE:

Vast Conquests

Despite Europe's small size, it was once able to conquer the world. Much of the continents of Asia and Africa were gobbled up by European countries. France, Germany, Britain, and other European countries laid claim to entire continents. Britain's colonial empire was the largest. By the 1800s, Europeans were colonizing places with huge populations and sophisticated civilizations—places like China, India, Africa, and the Middle East. By 1900, they were so advanced that no nation on earth could stand up to them. Britain, France, Italy, Germany, Spain, the Dutch, and most other European countries had developed massive, iron warships armed with tremendous cannons. These ships were capable of blowing apart older, wooden ships in a few shots. Guns had also continued to develop as well. Most

European armies were equipped with some sort of automatic rifles and mounted machine guns. This meant it only took small amounts of soldiers to conquer huge places.

CRYPTOGRAM: THE VASTNESS OF THE BRITISH EMPIRE

(Activity Book page 137)

Britain's colonial empire was the largest. It was so vast that there was a saying about the daytime in British territories around the globe. What was this saying?

Answer: THE SUN NEVER SETS ON THE BRITISH EMPIRE

CROSSWORD PUZZLE: CONTROLLING THE FAR EAST

(Activity Book page 138)

Answer Key:

Across:

  6. Boxers

  7. Taiyuan

Down:

  1. five

  2. fists

  3. Yangtze

  4. Beijing

  5. dollars

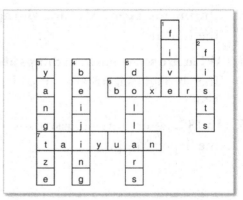

CRAFT PROJECT: MAKE A CHINESE HAT

Materials:

- ☐ Large sheet of colored poster board
- ☐ Scissors
- ☐ Tape
- ☐ Glue
- ☐ Markers

Instructions:

1. Cut a large circle out of the poster board.
2. Cut a slit from the edge of the circle toward the center. Stop at the center.
3. Bring the circle together into a cone shape. At this point, you can see where you will need to glue it.
4. After gluing the cone, tape it for extra reinforcement.
5. Decorate your hat with Chinese symbols (you can find common ones online).

SNACK PROJECT: BRITISH CANDY BOATS ON THE YANGTZE RIVER

Materials and Ingredients:

- ☐ Candied fruit slices
- ☐ Toothpicks
- ☐ Colored pencils
- ☐ Tape
- ☐ 1 tub Cool Whip
- ☐ Blue food coloring
- ☐ Templates from Activity Book *(Activity Book page 139)*

Instructions:
1. Cut out and color the twelve small British flags from the Activity Book.
2. Tape each flag to the top of a toothpick.
3. Insert one flag into each fruit slice, creating a boat.
4. Place Cool Whip in a bowl.
5. Add a few drops of blue food coloring. Stir with spatula.
6. Transfer the cool whip into a baking dish to make the Yangtze River.
7. Place the British ships on the river.
8. Enjoy!

CHAPTER 27
THE GREAT WAR

QUESTIONS FOR REVIEW:

1. **What countries belonged to the Allies during World War I?**
   Britain, France, and Italy.

2. **What countries belonged to the Central Powers?**
   The German Empire, the Austro-Hungarian Empire, and the Ottoman Empire.

3. **What was World War I also known as?**
   The Great War.

4. **During what years was World War I fought?**
   1914 to 1918.

5. **What caused the Americans to join the war?**
   The Germans sunk a ship that was carrying passengers from the United States. Germany was afraid and tried to encourage Mexico to attack the United States, which only provoked US involvement even more.

NARRATION EXERCISE:

The Great War / World War I

World War I was fought from 1914 to 1918. This was going to be a new kind of war. Technology had developed a lot over the past few decades. The armies of World War I were equipped with machine guns, grenades, submarines, poison gas, and many more new tools that made war deadlier than it had ever been. In the summer of 1914, the German armies tried to invade France. The fighting was much harder than anyone expected. With machine guns capable of firing hundreds of bullets at a time, armies couldn't just stand in rows and face each other like in the old days. The French and German armies dug trenches and hid in them and continued firing at each other from these long holes. And they stayed there and fought for years. It was very difficult for either side to gain ground. The land around the trenches became muddy wastelands, and the grass and trees were destroyed from all the explosions and fighting. Thousands of soldiers on both sides were killed.

MAP ACTIVITY: THE ALLIES AND CENTRAL POWERS

(Activity Book page 141) (see page 260 in your text book for help)

1. Color the countries of Britain, France, Russia, Italy, and the United States blue. These represent the Allies during World War I.

2. Color Germany, Austria-Hungary, Bulgaria, and the Ottoman Empire red. These were the Central Powers.

3. Find the dot representing Sarajevo. Circle it and draw a small gun next to it. Above the gun, write "June 28, 1914." This signifies the assassination place and date of Archduke Franz Ferdinand, the crown prince of the Austro-Hungarian Empire, which started the Great War.

DOUBLE PUZZLE: THE ASSASSINATION OF ARCHDUKE FERDINAND

(Activity Book page 142)

Unscramble the words from the section "The Assassination of Archduke Ferdinand." Copy the letters in the numbered blocks to the blocks with the corresponding numbers at the bottom to help answer the question.

Where did the first sparks of World War I occur?

Answer Key:

Gavrilo Princip

Serbs

Archduke Ferdinand

Duchess Sophie

Russia

Kaiser Wilhelm

Germans

France

The Austro-Hungarian Empire

LIAGOVR CINRIPP	G A V R I L O P R I N C I P
SEBRS	S E R B S
KEUAHDRC FARNDIDEN	A R C H D U K E F E R D I N A N D
SUCDESH SOEPIH	D U C H E S S S O P H I E
SAIRSU	R U S S I A
ERSAKI WLMHILE	K A I S E R W I L H E L M
GNSEARM	G E R M A N S
CEANFR	F R A N C E

CRAFT PROJECT: WORLD WAR I AIRPLANE

Materials:

- ☐ Cardboard pieces
- ☐ 1 empty toilet paper roll or paper towel roll cut in half
- ☐ Scissors or utility knife
- ☐ Glue
- ☐ Colored markers
- ☐ Templates from Activity Book *(Activity Book page 143)*

Instructions:

1. Color and cut out the airplane wings, tail, and propeller from the Activity Book.
2. Use these to trace onto cardboard.
3. Using the toilet paper roll as the body, cut slits in the center to insert the wings.
4. Glue on the tail and the propeller.
5. Let it dry.
6. Decorate.

CRAFT PROJECT: THE BRITISH TRENCHES

Materials:

- ☐ Medium-size cardboard box
- ☐ Toothpicks
- ☐ Craft sticks
- ☐ Glue or tape
- ☐ Mud or potting soil
- ☐ Twigs from outside
- ☐ Plastic army men (optional)

Instructions:
1. Create the trenches in the cardboard box using slightly moistened dirt, just enough to form the trenches so they stand up. It is important not to make it too moist or it will not hold together.
2. After the trenches are created, line the walls using craft sticks by pushing them lightly into the muddy sides. Not all the walls need to be covered.
3. Using the toothpicks and glue, create ladders to put all around the trenches.
4. Put twigs around the tops of the trenches to look like trees.
5. Place army men in the trenches.

CHAPTER 28
THE RISE OF THE DICTATORS

QUESTIONS FOR REVIEW:

1. **What was the purpose of the Treaty of Versailles?**
    To punish Germany by taking away territory and limiting the size of their army and to make them pay for the cost of the war.

2. **Who were Fascists against?**
    Communists.

3. **Who was the Italian Fascist leader?**
    Benito Mussolini.

4. **Who was the leader of the Nazis in Germany?**
    Adolf Hitler.

5. **What country is the USSR?**
    Russia.

NARRATION EXERCISES:

The Treaty of Versailles
The Treaty of Versailles punished Germany by taking away German territory and limiting the size of Germany's army. The Treaty of Versailles also made the Germans pay for the whole cost of the war. The German people were humiliated by the Treaty of Versailles. It made them weak and vulnerable. They found it unfair and felt taken advantage of.

Mussolini and the Blackshirts
From 1919 to 1920, it looked like the Kingdom of Italy would become Communist. Many Italians were afraid of living under Communist rule. Some wanted to fight Communist violence with violence of their own. These people were called the Fascists. *Fascists* wanted a very strong national government and a leader who

would suppress opposition and free speech. The Fascists wore black in public and were known as Blackshirts. The leader of the Italian Fascists was a newspaper publisher named Benito Mussolini. Mussolini was a powerful speaker who held huge rallies attended by thousands of Fascists. King Victor Emmanuel's counselors recommended he make Mussolini prime minister. So in 1922, he invited Mussolini to come to Rome and become prime minister, but Mussolini wielded so much power and influence that many looked at him as dictator of Italy. Mussolini changed everything in Italy. He got rid of local mayors and city councils and replaced them with Fascist officials. He brought companies under control of the government, abolished free elections, and only allowed newspapers to write good things about him. People who resisted Mussolini could be imprisoned or killed. One thing Mussolini accomplished was making peace between the Catholic Church and Italy. In 1929, Mussolini and Pope Pius XI signed the Lateran Treaty, in which Mussolini recognized the independence of the pope, and the pope recognized the Italian state.

WORD SEARCH: HITLER

(Activity Book pages 145-146)

Fill in the blanks for the Hitler word search clues and then find the corresponding words in the word search.

Answer Key:

1. Germany
2. race
3. Jewish
4. Nazis
5. control
6. revolution
7. arrested
8. violence
9. chancellor
10. dictator

```
R E F Q M Q F R O C X J P B C
V O R S R R L N E P E L K C J
F I L A X P E J H W I O T S P
I Z W L G N D J I Z R A X V D
C X Y A E V G S D I X I N T E
F W P O S C H E X K X T T E T
C A M P Q U N A R T I Q Y X S
O H N C C X J A R M K C N E E
N I K Q R U J V H Y A Q C E R
T M C I E W F H I C H N O T R
R S I Z A N U P N E E P Y F A
O C E O N O I T U L O V E R L
L B J C K E G I O P X J Y U C
R R T D A D D I C T A T O R U
J V S H I R V S D C U T U G O
```

CRAFT PROJECT: TREATY OF VERSAILLES DOCUMENT

Materials:

☐ Brown paper bag

☐ Black marker

☐ Scissors

Instructions:

1. Cut out a large rectangle from the blank side of the paper bag.
2. Using large letters, write "The Treaty of Versailles" on the top.
3. On the next line write, "This document hereby states that Germany . . ."
4. Proceed to make a list of all the things that the treaty required Germany to do.
5. Review them together and discuss how upset this must have made the German people.

CRAFT PROJECT: MAKE A MINI FASCES

Materials:

☐ 1 dowel, ½″ diameter and about 1 ½′ long

☐ 9–12 dowels, ¼″ diameter and about 1′ long

☐ Hot glue gun

☐ Red ribbon

☐ Small piece of cardboard

☐ Scissors

☐ Tape

☐ Silver spray paint

Instructions:

1. Put glue along one of the ¼″ dowels and place it along the side of the ½″ dowel. Save space at the bottom of the ½″ dowel to be used as a handle.
2. Continue to do this for each ¼″ dowel until all are placed around the ½″ dowel.
3. Let dry.
4. Prepare the ax blade by cutting the shape of the blade out of cardboard. Any size blade is fine.

5. Spraypaint the ax blade with the silver spray paint.

6. Let dry.

7. Use red ribbon to wrap around the fasces as a decoration. It does not need to be covered completely with the ribbon.

8. Insert the dried ax blade into the top/center of the fasces. You might need to tape it in or glue it again.

CHAPTER 29
THE SECOND WORLD WAR

QUESTIONS FOR REVIEW:

1. **What was another name for the Nazis?**
   The Third Reich.

2. **What is the League of Nations?**
   A group of countries that formed together to prevent war and talk out problems peacefully.

3. **What were the years of the Second World War?**
   1939 to 1945.

4. **What did Hitler and the Nazis do to those who resisted them?**
   Those who opposed the Nazis were killed or sent to concentration camps.

5. **What battle prompted the beginning of the end for Nazi Germany?**
   The Battle of Stalingrad.

NARRATION EXERCISE:

Hitler and the Third Reich

Hitler did not want to participate in the League of Nations and removed Germany from it. He also broke the Treaty of Versailles, enlarging the German army beyond what the treaty allowed. The Nazis began persecuting the Jews, forbidding them from taking part in the government, stripping them of certain rights, and even using violence against them. Hitler also had plans to make the Third Reich the biggest, most powerful nation on earth. To do this, he wanted everywhere Germans were living to become part of the Third Reich. In 1938, Hitler annexed Austria to Germany and joined the two countries together. Still, the Allies did nothing. The British prime minister Neville Chamberlain went to negotiate with Hitler. Hitler promised Chamberlain that if the league would only give him Czechoslovakia, he would be happy. Reluctantly, the League of Nations agreed, and Hitler's tanks rolled into Czechoslovakia. Chamberlain came back to England, waving the piece of paper Hitler had signed, saying the agreement meant "peace for our time." Hitler, however, did not want peace. He wanted war. He broke his promise. Within a year, German tanks invaded Poland, and Britain and France declared war on Germany. This was the beginning of the Second World War, which lasted from 1939 to 1945.

CROSSWORD PUZZLE: THE SECOND WORLD WAR

(Activity Book page 147)

Answer Key:

Across:

4. Chamberlain

5. battle

6. nations

8. Blitzkrieg

Down:

1. concentration

2. France

3. Reich

7. Jews

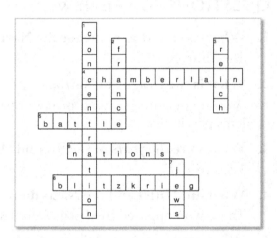

CRAFT PROJECT: 2D PAPER ARMY TANK

Materials:

☐ Scissors

☐ Glue

☐ Colored markers or pencils

☐ A piece of construction paper (any color)

☐ Template from Activity Book *(Activity Book page 149)*

Instructions:

1. Color and cut out the tank pieces for the army tank in the Activity Book.
2. See if you can figure out which pieces go where using the numbers for help. Your finished product should look like the tank shown here.
3. Enjoy your tank!

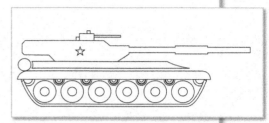

SNACK PROJECT: CANDY TANK

Materials and Ingredients:

☐ 6 mini Reese's Peanut Butter Cups, wrapped

☐ Tootsie Roll Pop, wrapped

☐ 2 mini Hershey candy bars, wrapped

☐ 3 Twix candy bars, wrapped

☐ Tape

Instructions:

1. Tape the Twix bars together to form the body of the tank.
2. Tape the peanut butter cups around, three on each side of the tank for the wheels.
3. Tape the mini candy bars on top in the middle of the tank.
4. Tape the Tootsie Roll Pop on the top of the mini candy bars, facing the stick outward as the barrel of the gun.
5. Enjoy your tank!

CHAPTER 30
THE THIRD REICH COLLAPSES

QUESTIONS FOR REVIEW:

1. **What did the Nazis do to the Jews around 1942?**
   The Nazis began the extermination of the Jews (genocide).

2. **What brave thing did St. Maximilian Kolbe do while inside a concentration camp?**
   He died in the place of a man who had a wife and family.

3. **What happened on December 7, 1941?**
   The Japanese attacked Pearl Harbor, killing more than two thousand American sailors.

4. **What is the name given to June 6, 1944, when the invasion of Normandy occurred?**
   D-Day.

5. **During what year did the Germans surrender, ending World War II?**
   1945.

NARRATION EXERCISE:

St. Maximilian Kolbe
In Poland, the Franciscan priest Maximilian Kolbe was arrested for publishing anti-Nazi writings. He was sent to the infamous Auschwitz concentration camp. While in Auschwitz, he was beaten severely for being a priest. In July 1941, some prisoners were sentenced to be killed. One of the men begged to be spared. "I have a wife and a family!" he cried. But the Nazi guards were unsympathetic. Father Kolbe stepped forward, saying, "Please, take me instead of him." The commander allowed the other man to go free. Father Maximilian Kolbe and several other prisoners were locked in a room to starve to death. Kolbe lived for two weeks, consoling the other prisoners. He was the last to die, killed by a poison injection

because the Nazis were sick of waiting for him to die. Maximilian Kolbe was regarded as a martyr and was later canonized. Today, he is one of the Church's most beloved saints.

CRAFT PROJECT: MAXIMILIAN KOLBE FIGURINE

Materials:

- ☐ Ping-pong ball
- ☐ Toilet paper roll
- ☐ Black and white poster paint
- ☐ Brown and black Sharpie markers
- ☐ Tape or glue

Instructions:

1. Use the brown Sharpie to draw a face with hair, a beard, and a mustache on the ping-pong ball.
2. Use the black Sharpie to draw two eyes and circular glasses around the eyes.
3. Paint the toilet paper roll with black and white stripes to resemble the concentration camp uniform.
4. Attach the head to the body with tape or glue.

CRAFT PROJECT: PARACHUTE FOR TOY ARMY MAN

Materials:

- ☐ Plastic grocery bag
- ☐ String or yarn
- ☐ Scissors
- ☐ Ruler
- ☐ Toy army man

Instructions:
1. Cut 2 6" pieces of string or yarn.
2. Thread one string through a grocery bag handle. Repeat with the other string and the other grocery bag handle.
3. Using the loose ends of the strings, tie the army man onto the parachute (by his arms or tie the strings around his waist).
4. Tape the strings to the army man if needed.
5. Toss him in the air and watch him parachute down!

WORD SEARCH: THE THIRD REICH COLLAPSES

(Activity Book page 151)

Find all the words related to the demise of the Nazis.

Answer Key:

1. Germans
2. Normandy
3. Japan
4. Pearl Harbor
5. Kolbe
6. Auschwitz
7. Hawaii
8. Roosevelt
9. France
10. survivors

```
A Q S K J K V I D P D B K R T
N U X N O A I Y D N A M R O N
E M S L A A P G K Y K M O O W
A J B C W M V A S R P V B S Q
D E O A H W R U N G X Q R E N
L Z H Z X W R E N X S E A V N
U P I W P V I D G D K K H E R
Y A K E I A E T D R T Q L L M
K S A V A Z J Y Z V K B R T O
U J O F R A N C E G Q G A Y X
Q R U W N S Z A E S I H E S N
S L I R R W J Q X F S Y P L R
B B C O H U V S B D A O G N F
G V D S F T B V F D F Z L O S
H D V J J B S T G S H V R H D
```

CHAPTER 31
THE COLD WAR

QUESTIONS FOR REVIEW:

1. **What did the United States do to try to stop World War II and the fighting with Japan?**
   They dropped two atomic bombs on the cities of Hiroshima and Nagasaki.

2. **What was the name of the war between Russia and the United States?**
   The Cold War.

3. **What were the countries of Russia and the United States referred to as?**
   Superpowers.

4. **What did the Germans build in order to keep people from escaping East Germany?**
   The Berlin Wall.

5. **What was the name given to the secret police of Russia who spied on people and punished opponents of the government?**
   The Stasi.

NARRATION EXERCISE:

The Cold War

In the closing days of World War II, United States scientists and military officials invented a new weapon called the atomic bomb. Since the Japanese continued fighting through the summer of 1945 and gave no signs of giving up, the United States decided to drop its atomic bombs on the Japanese cities of Hiroshima and Nagasaki. Japan surrendered right away, bringing an end to the war in the Pacific. But Joseph Stalin wanted the atomic bomb for himself. Russian scientists in the Soviet Union were working around the clock to discover how to build their own. In 1949, the Soviet Union announced that it had built and tested its own atomic bomb. Now Russia and the United States *both* had atomic bombs. The Americans began developing more and bigger nuclear weapons, and the Soviets did the same. The two countries thus tried to outmaneuver each other, but without getting into an actual war. This time period was called the Cold War. The *Cold War* refers to a long period of tension between the United States and the Soviet Union. The two superpowers never declared war on each other, but they competed indirectly in a number of ways and tried to oppose each other in any way they could.

MAP ACTIVITY: RUSSIA'S IRON CURTAIN

(Activity Book page 152)

1. Trace the dotted line that represents Russia's Iron Curtain with a black marker to show how it ripped Europe in half.
2. Color everything behind the Iron Curtain (east) red to show the extent of the Soviet's control.
3. Color everything on the other side of the Iron Curtain (west) blue.
4. Circle the city of Berlin and write the word "Wall" above it to note the Berlin Wall and show the edge of the Iron Curtain.
5. On the east side of the word "Wall," write "Communist East," then write "Free Democratic West" on the other side.

DOUBLE PUZZLE: THE COLD WAR

(Activity Book page 153)

Unscramble the words from this chapter. Copy the letters in the numbered blocks to the blocks with the corresponding numbers at the bottom to answer the question.

The United States dropped atomic bombs on what two Japanese cities?

Answer Key:

Russia	The Cold War
Superpowers	Germany
Japan	Berlin Wall
Nuclear	**Nagasaki and**
Atomic	**Hiroshima**

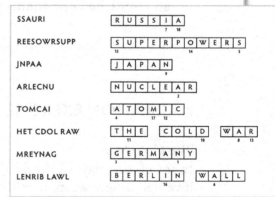

CRAFT PROJECT: ARMY DOG TAG

Materials:

- ☐ Rectangular key chain
- ☐ String or yarn
- ☐ A small photo of yourself
- ☐ Glue
- ☐ Scissors

Instructions:

1. Have a picture taken of yourself, small enough to fit onto the keychain. (You can change the size of it on your computer imaging program.)
2. Cut out the picture and glue it onto the keychain.
3. Attach the string to the keychain.
4. Your army tag is ready to wear.

SNACK PROJECT: A CANDY BERLIN WALL

Materials:

- ☐ Mamba candies
- ☐ Vanilla frosting
- ☐ Paper plate

Instructions:

1. Build a brick wall by stacking the Mamba candies with frosting between each.
2. Use about six or seven Mamba candies for each row.
3. Make about seven rows, alternating the stacking of candy as you would for bricks.
4. You can smash part of the Berlin Wall, imitating when it came down.

CRAFT PROJECT: ARMY NURSE HAT (FOR GIRLS)

Materials:

☐ Tape or glue stick

☐ Scissors

☐ Red marker

☐ 8.5x11 sheet of white paper

☐ Folding instructions and template from Activity Book *(Activity Book page 154-155)*

Instructions:

1. Follow the visual origami folding instructions to make a nurse's hat in the Activity Book.

2. Color and cut out the cross template for the nurse's hat in the Activity Book.

3. Tape or glue the cross onto the hat.

CHAPTER 32
CHANGES IN THE MODERN WORLD

QUESTIONS FOR REVIEW:

1. **What brought news and entertainment into people's homes in the 1950s?**
   Television.

2. **What is it called when the government takes control of an industry such as electricity or telephone service?**
   Nationalization.

3. **What are some things that new technology made easier?**
   Communication, medical care, better treatment for disease, and better quality of life.

4. **What does hedonism mean?**
   Living for the pursuit of pleasure.

5. **During this period, how was Christianity viewed in the Communist east and in the free west?**
   It was outlawed in the Communist East and ridiculed or mocked in the free West.

NARRATION EXERCISE:

A New Way of Living
The monarchies of old Christendom had been swept away after World War I. By the twentieth century, Christendom was little more than a dream. In the 1950s and '60s, new technology was altering the way people lived. A new invention, the television set, allowed people to watch television programs and news right in their own homes. Also, more people than ever were buying cars, and modern appliances were invented to make household life easier, such as microwaves, refrigerators, and washers and dryers. After World War II, European governments sometimes took control of the electricity or telephone service in order to set it up the way they

wanted. Engineers in the United States and Britain were working on new devices for processing and storing data; these were the first computers. New technology also made communication easier and made things like medical care better; people were living longer, getting better treatment for disease, and enjoying a better quality of life.

CRAFT PROJECT: MINI 1950S TELEVISION SET

Materials:

- ☐ An empty Keurig box or similar (the smallest size)
- ☐ 4 clip-on clothespins
- ☐ 2 twist ties
- ☐ Scissors
- ☐ Tape
- ☐ Brown poster paint
- ☐ Black Sharpie marker
- ☐ Any small picture to fit into the television screen

Instructions:

1. Cut out the entire rectangular section of the box where you would normally open the flap to take out the coffee pods. This opening will be the base or the bottom of the television set. Place the cut-out part facedown on the table.

2. The section now facing you will be the television screen. Cut out an inner rectangle piece from this section to make an opening for the screen.

3. Paint the entire television with brown poster paint. Let dry. Draw television knobs with black Sharpie.

4. Tape any picture onto the inside of the screen.

5. Attach the four clothespins underneath the opening you first made to make it stand up.

6. Tape the two twist ties to the top for the antenna.

CRAFT PROJECT: HANDMADE TELEPHONE

Materials:

- ☐ 2 Solo plastic cups
- ☐ 7–10 feet of yarn
- ☐ Scissors
- ☐ 2 paper clips

Instructions:

1. Poke a hole in the bottom of each cup.
2. Thread the yarn into the hole on one cup.
3. Tie a knot with the yarn onto the paper clip on the outside bottom side of the cup.
4. Repeat steps 1–3 for the second cup using the other end of the yarn.
5. Your homemade telephone is ready to use!

CRYPTOGRAM: CHANGES IN THE MODERN WORLD

(Activity Book page 157)

With progress comes the temptation to forget about God and the laws He established. The modern age with all its technologies and conveniences had no time for God. As a result, Church attendance dropped across Europe. Even if people did not become outright atheists, many lived as if God did not exist. What did all of this lead to?

Answer: The Decay of Morals

CROSSWORD PUZZLE: A NEW WAY OF LIVING

(Activity Book page 158)

Answer Key:

Across:

  3. computer

  4. nationalism

  5. Italian

  7. one

Down:

  1. technology

  2. appliances

  6. three

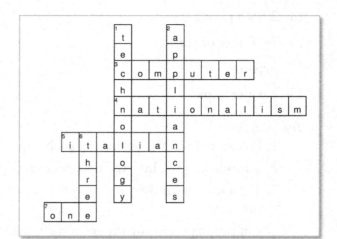

CHAPTER 33
THE SECOND VATICAN COUNCIL

QUESTIONS FOR REVIEW:

1. **In 1962, Pope John XXIII asked bishops all over the world to do what?**
   Submit ideas about the Church to discuss at the Second Vatican Council.

2. **The Second Vatican Council reminded Catholics that what was for everybody?**
   Holiness.

3. **What did the Second Vatican Council request concerning the Mass?**
   It requested a reform of the liturgical books the Church uses at Mass.

4. **After the council ended, who formed a special commission to reform the sacred liturgy?**
   Pope Paul VI.

5. **What was it like for Catholics years after the council?**
   Chaotic and confusing.

NARRATION EXERCISE:

Second Vatican Council
Pope John XXIII believed that the Church needed to update its message for the new age and wanted to summon an ecumenical council to do this. He asked bishops from all over the world to submit ideas to discuss at a council. The bishops responded enthusiastically, recommending everything from stronger condemnations of Communism, to a reform of the liturgy, to a clarification on the Church's teaching on marriage. Pope John XXIII summoned the Second Vatican Council in the fall of 1962. Pope John died before the council ended, but his vision

was carried on by the new pope, Paul VI. The council taught that the Church is the people of God, and it reminded Catholics that holiness is for everybody. It encouraged Catholics to participate in the liturgy prayerfully and studiously, and it suggested that in a world where so many people did not believe in God, it would be better for Catholics and Protestants to focus on what unites them rather than on what divides them. After the council ended, Pope Paul VI formed a special commission to reform the sacred liturgy. The result was the "New Order of the Mass," which was set to become the new Mass of the Church in 1970.

WORD SEARCH: THE SECOND VATICAN COUNCIL

(Activity Book page 159)

Find all the words related to this historic church council.

Answer Key:

1. Novus Ordo
2. council
3. Vatican
4. Communism
5. confusion
6. liturgy
7. Pope Paul
8. reform
9. bishops

```
L I T U R G Y B C I Y H N D S
I Q R J U E S V I B S O J N E
N O D R P F R E A S F H A E E
L O N Z W F E K P U H C Q D X
U Z I E U H F F S O I O P P L
A F O S F W O B C T P T P F I
P N T D U G R T A Y X D Y S C
E P R Q K F M V P I Z R D Z N
P K N F A Y N S T N R A B S U
O G O Y E U O O N D F U L Q O
P F G D Y W E A C M A O J E C
V L C C V L J T Z A Y L W S F
W N O V U S O R D O J F Z L Q
O S D D N M X N G R K I I L L
H K N O D M M S I N U M M O C
```

DOUBLE PUZZLE: THE SECOND VATICAN COUNCIL

(Activity Book page 161)

Unscramble the words from this chapter. Copy the letters in the numbered blocks to the blocks with the corresponding numbers at the bottom to help answer the question.

What was the Latin name for the new Mass that resulted from the Second Vatican Council?

Answer Key:

Vatican

Council

Paul

Pius

John

Latin

Chant

Catholics

Bishops

Novus Ordo Missae

VINCATA	V A T I C A N
CULCOIN	C O U N C I L
PULA	P A U L
IPSU	P I U S
HJNO	J O H N
LAINT	L A T I N
NAHCT	C H A N T
HCLOTSAIC	C A T H O L I C S
PISBOHS	B I S H O P S

SNACK PROJECT: GIANT RICE KRISPIES TREAT BISHOP'S MITER

Materials and Ingredients:

☐ Rice Krispies treat recipe

☐ Wax paper

☐ Knife

☐ Ruler

☐ Premade can of white cake frosting (1 or 2 cans)

☐ Yellow food coloring

Instructions:

1. Prepare the Rice Krispies treats and spread it evenly on wax paper. Let cool.

2. Using a ruler as a guide, cut a giant pentagon shape out of the Rice Krispies treats. This is the bishop's miter.

3. Transfer it to another sheet of wax paper or a pan large enough to fit it.

4. Frost the entire miter with white frosting. Save about two tablespoons.

5. Color the leftover two tablespoons of frosting yellow.

6. With the yellow frosting, decorate the center of the miter with a cross.

7. Enjoy!

CHAPTER 34
THE END OF THE COLD WAR

QUESTIONS FOR REVIEW:

1. **Who was elected pope in 1978 after Pope John Paul served only a few weeks?**
   Pope John Paul II.

2. **What did the pope believe the problem of the world was?**
   That man had forgotten about God.

3. **What happened to the pope on May 13, 1981?**
   The pope was shot in an attempt to assassinate him.

4. **What other important event of history had happened on May 13?**
   Mary came to visit three shepherd children in Fatima.

5. **What happened to the Berlin Wall that separated East Germany from West Germany?**
   People began smashing it with hammers and tearing it down, making Germany united and free again.

NARRATION EXERCISE:

Karol Wojtyla / Pope St. John Paul II
Karol Wojtyla was the archbishop of Cracow, Poland, and was elected to the papacy in 1978 after his predecessor, John Paul, died just a few weeks after being elected. Karol took the name John Paul II to honor the man who came before him. At age fifty-eight, John Paul II was one of the youngest men to be elected pope. He was also the first non-Italian pope in more than four hundred years and the very first pope from Poland. He traveled all over the world during his papacy and spoke to millions of people. One of the things John Paul II was most known for was how he took on Communism. Some think this was the reason someone tried to take his life on May 13, 1981, when a Turkish assassin shot him in St. Peter's

Square. John Paul II would survive this shooting and later find its date meaning-ful, since May 13 was the date Mary visited the three shepherd children in Fatima. In response to his life being spared, he thanked Mary and consecrated the world to her Immaculate Heart on March 25, 1984, the Feast of the Annunciation.

MAZE

(Activity Book page 162)
Help the Germans get over and across the Berlin Wall.

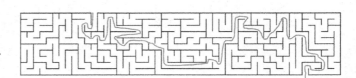

CRYPTOGRAM: JOHN PAUL II

(Activity Book page 163)
Pope John Paul II was a new kind of pope. In his first words to the Catholic Church and the people of the word, Pope John Paul II spoke about not being afraid and accepting Christ.
What were some of his words?
Answer: Open Wide the Doors for Christ

SNACK PROJECT: TWIX CANDY BERLIN WALL

Materials:

☐ Bag of mini Twix candy bars

☐ Frosting

☐ Paper plate

☐ Sharp cutting knife or meat mallet

Instructions:
1. Build the Berlin Wall to the size of your liking by stacking the Twix bars, using frosting as glue.
2. After it has set, carefully cut a jagged section out with a sharp knife, to resemble the broken Berlin Wall. Or, smash the wall with a meat mallet.
3. Enjoy!

CRAFT PROJECT: POPE JOHN PAUL II PAPER BAG PUPPET

Materials:

☐ White paper lunch/craft bag

☐ Scissors

☐ Glue

☐ Yellow and red markers

☐ Templates from Activity Book *(Activity Book page 165–167)*

Instructions:

1. Cut out the template for the John Paul II head and zucchetto in Activity Book.
2. Glue the head to the top of the paper bag where it is folded. This will be the head of the puppet.
3. Glue the zucchetto to the top of the head.
4. Draw and color a red "cape" around the "shoulders" of the puppet.
5. Draw a yellow necklace with a crucifix coming out of the "cape."
6. The Pope John Paul II puppet is ready to use!

CHAPTER 35
AN UNCERTAIN FUTURE

QUESTIONS FOR REVIEW:

1. **What did Pope John Paul II do to try to fix the chaos in the Catholic Church after the Second Vatican Council?**
   He published the "Catechism of the Catholic Church."

2. **How long was John Paul II pope?**
   Twenty-seven years.

3. **What year did Pope John Paul II die?**
   2005.

4. **What other works were written by Pope John Paul II?**
   He wrote many important documents about the Eucharist, marriage, and the liturgy.

5. **What caused Christendom to fracture and fall apart?**
   The sins and failures of men.

NARRATION EXERCISE:

Modern Europe
John Paul had worked hard to bring reform to the Church. Since there had been so much fighting and division in Europe over the past century, people wanted more harmony. If Europeans could work together on economic and political problems, Europe would be a more peaceful place. In 1993, several countries joined together to form the European Union, or the EU. Its original members were Germany, France, Italy, Netherlands, Belgium, and Luxembourg. Since 1993, twenty-two more European countries have joined. That's not to say there haven't still been problems. Wars broke out in the Balkans, Protestants and Catholics were still fighting in Ireland, and civil war has torn Ukraine apart. Many Europeans have also had a hard time finding jobs. In some countries, taxes are so high it's difficult

to get by; in others, the governments are almost bankrupt. Another problem is population. European parents are having fewer and fewer children. Though St. John Paul II and his successors have done many good things for the Church, Christianity in Europe is at a crossroads. Mass attendance is low and Christianity is a small religion in countries where it used to be dominant. Europe is presently struggling with her identity.

WORD SEARCH: AN UNCERTAIN FUTURE

(Activity Book page 169)

Find all the words related to this chapter.

Answer Key:

1. Europe
2. catechism
3. mosque
4. Euro
5. Ireland
6. Germany
7. Italy
8. immigrants
9. Christendom

CRAFT PROJECT: CATECHISM OF THE CATHOLIC CHURCH MINI BOOK

Materials:

☐ 8 ½" × 11" copy paper

☐ Colored pencils

☐ Scissors

Instructions:

1. Place the paper in front of you with the vertical (long) side going upward.
2. Fold it in half. Rub the creases of the fold with the edge of the scissors.
3. Fold it in half two more times. Continue to rub the creases of the folds. By now the paper should appear to be in the shape of a book, about 4" × 2 ½".

4. Open up the folds two times until you are back in the original half fold as in step #2.

5. With the folded side facing you, cut the center folded vertical line up to the middle of the paper where all the folded lines intersect and stop.

6. Open the entire paper. There should be a slit in the very center of the paper.

7. You should now be able to push the sides together to form a mini book (about 4″ × 2 ½″) that has eight pages, including front cover and back page. The pages will appear to be double, but that is OK. No other cutting is necessary.

8. On the front of the book, write "Catechism of the Catholic Church."

9. On the inside of the book, write the following words on separate pages and draw a symbolic picture for each: *Faith, The Apostles' Creed, Scripture, Mystery, Sacraments, Commandments, The Lord's Prayer.*

10. Your mini Catechism book is finished!

CRAFT PROJECT: HOLY WATER FONT

Materials:

☐ A small, plain, rectangular wooden plaque

☐ Sawtooth picture hanger

☐ Hammer

☐ Clear plastic shot glass

☐ School glue

☐ Hot glue gun and glue sticks

☐ Holy card picture

Instructions:

1. Install the picture hanger to the back of the wooden plaque (parents might have to help).

2. Use the school glue to paste the holy card onto the front of the plaque, saving a small space at the bottom for the cup to hang. You may cut the holy card to fit.

3. Install the plastic shot glass using the hot glue gun. This should be glued near at the bottom of the plaque where you left empty space under the holy card picture.

4. Let dry.

5. Hang to wall and add holy water.